Personal
Power

Other books by Philippa Davies, also published by Piatkus:

Total Confidence: The complete guide to self-assurance and personal success

Your Total Image: How to communicate success

Philippa Davies

Personal Power

How to become more **assertive**

and **successful** at work

PIATKUS

To Alyson Spiro, Maureen O'Donnell,
Meryl Griffiths and Michael Pokorny

First published in 1991 by
Judy Piatkus (Publishers) Ltd,
5 Windmill Street, London W1P 1HF

First paperback edition 1992
Reprinted 1994
Revised edition 1996
First published in hardcover as
Status: What it is and how to achieve it

A catalogue record for this book is available from the British Library

ISBN 0–7499–1642–7 (Pbk)

Cover design by Ken Leeder
Designed by Paul Saunders
Edited by Esther Jagger

Typeset in 11/13 pt Linotron Sabon by
Wyvern Typesetting Ltd, Bristol
Printed and bound in Great Britain by
The Bath Press, Bath, Avon

CONTENTS

INTRODUCTION

Since this book was first published, my colleagues and I have included practical work on personal power on many of our training courses and coaching sessions. We have been fascinated at how people react to the subject, initially expressing embarrassment and discomfort, followed by relief and a willingness to disclose a great deal as discussion continues. We have learned that in many organisations the way in which people use power in a role is a completely taboo area. We have realised, too, that for many individuals their own use of power is a much more sensitive topic than, say, their sex lives. Above all, it has made me understand that many of us seek personal power, but would be very reluctant to admit it.

Writing *Personal Power* was not an entirely comfortable experience. All too often I was reminded of my own awkward and embarrassing attempts at increasing my power in certain situations. It made me smile to reflect how often we play power games during our everyday social interaction – and how much these stabs at power are part of our human make-up.

Personal Power is about how we regard ourselves and how other people regard us. Starting with ourselves, it considers self-esteem and the values, hidden agendas and tactics we use in dealing with one another. It looks at how we use and develop different approaches to influencing others – non-verbal signals, clothes and speech can all reflect personal power.

I will also show you how to increase your visibility, so that you can gain recognition and publicity for your professional skills, your business, or a cause to which you are committed. Finally, I will investigate the idea of 'status' – what it means in our society and the systems through which it operates. Though we may feel uncomfortable with the idea, status very often results from having a large amount of personal power.

I hope that reading this book will deepen your understanding of personal power and help you to use it well and with integrity in both your professional and your personal life.

Philippa Davies

chapter one

GIVING YOURSELF
POWER

ersonal Power is about making things happen. It's to do with getting your own needs fulfilled, and helping others get what they want. It's about aspiring to realise your own potential, while maintaining integrity in your dealings with others. It is about striving for an ideal – and knowing that ideals matter. Ideals are important because they give us, both as individuals and as members of society, a sense of vision and direction. When we hold on to ideals, we become inspired and motivated by 'what might be'.

One meaning of power is energy. When we lack personal power we feel angry, frustrated or lethargic; our energy distorts into tension or ebbs away altogether. We become victims of circumstance, and lack the energy to take responsibility for our predicament. We have no impetus to make things happen. You possibly recognise this feeling.

In this situation, first of all we need to look at ourselves, and then at how we are interacting with other people and external circumstances. Personal power is created and fuelled by a sense of self-esteem. There is no point learning to use assertive and influential behaviour if you really don't believe that you deserve the rewards these skills can bring. When you try to do this, you can find that you unconsciously sabotage your own progress by perhaps taking the wrong decisions, martyring yourself for others, or feeling responsible for people and events that are outside your control. Lack of self-esteem is an extremely powerful undermining force.

People often become embarrassed or cynical when self-esteem is mentioned. They will quickly move on to another subject, or dismiss self-esteem as 'something Americans are always going on about'.

This denial of significance is, I think, to do with wanting to avoid pain and suffering. Who we are is determined by our genes and the sum of our experiences, especially those experiences we have with our close family. These experiences inevitably involve, for all of us, uncomfortable responses: the humiliation of shame, the anguish of guilt, the bitterness of envy. When we consider and tend to our self-esteem, we often have to acknowledge that life has not all been a bed of roses.

And when our self-esteem is low and we feel inadequate, those who champion the common-sense approach don't always help. Someone who themself has a fear of introspection and so avoids it and suggests you do the same, telling you to 'pull yourself together and do something' will not be helpful. Indeed, you may have neglected to consider and build your self-esteem because you have always been so busy 'doing'. A time for reflection and reappraisal can be just what you need.

It must be said, however, that a chapter in a book cannot give someone self-esteem and belief in themself overnight. What it *can* do is to offer explanation, understanding and suggestions for further development. And as reading is a quiet, reflective activity, I hope that my words on the page can help to stimulate you into reappraisal.

You will find that the benefits of gaining insight and self-esteem will far outweigh any discomfort you may experience in getting there. If you start immediately to regard yourself as somebody who has great potential for change and self-fulfilment, you are already on your way.

Before looking at the connection between personality and self-esteem, I should explain the standpoint from which I am writing this chapter. We are attracted to investigate what we need, and I have had to work hard to build my own self-esteem, first as an actress, later as a voice teacher, and now as a trainer of communication skills. Sometimes, especially when confronted with new challenges, my fragile level of self-esteem can still plummet, but I now have guidelines I follow which help to build me up again. Let me share them with you.

YOUR PERSONALITY AND POWER

What is 'personality'? Why are some people 'full of themselves' and others 'full of self-doubt'? These questions have preoccupied fine minds for centuries, with interest intensifying from the late nineteenth century to the present day. Two of the greatest theorists were Sigmund Freud, born in 1856, and Carl Jung, born in 1875. Freud is often referred to as the grandfather of psychoanalysis, and his research and theories changed the way we think about ourselves. Though it's fashionable in some quarters to 'knock Freud', he remains the yardstick from which others choose to deviate. Psychologists, analysts and therapists often hold strong fundamental allegiances to one set of theories or another, but then temper their views as they are influenced by other approaches. There is a huge amount to be read on the subject; if it interests you further, see the Reading List on p. 203.

The galling thing about 'what is personality?' is that there are no concrete answers and no absolute truth. We can only ask ourselves more questions, and the answers we supply will reflect our own psychology. We may assert that people are essentially good and born in a 'state of grace' because we need to convince ourselves of these facts. Deep down inside, our belief may be that on the whole we're a bad lot. To make a lofty comparison, critiques of Freud are invariably written from the perspective of an analysis of his theories viewed with modern psychological hindsight on the man himself. They will include comments like 'Freud himself was a sincere and generous man, as well as a genius' (David Stafford Clark, *What Freud Really Said*).

If, on the other hand you have an open mind, and want to understand yourself and other people, then an exciting discovery lies ahead. Your view of yourself and your potential and direction for development depend on your definition of personality. If you believe, for instance, that behaviour cannot be changed, and that it's 'unnatural' to do this, then there's no point in learning influencing or assertiveness skills. If, in defence of your own attitudes, you don't wish to examine them and believe that they are fixed, it's not worth exposing yourself and listening to anything that might make you think differently. In attempting to understand 'who you are', ask yourself the extent to which you consider your personality is determined by:

11

- Your genes: we can see that we inherit physical characteristics from our parents; some illnesses are also genetic. The extent to which personality is inherited is debatable. Some recent research has suggested that alcoholism may be genetically inherited – a high proportion of alcoholics have alcoholic parents. This could, of course, be affected by . . .

- Your early conditioning: the latest psychological fad in America is for pregnant women to talk to their babies while still in the womb. Apparently, if a baby kicks and is repeatedly given a response to that kick by touch, it can become highly responsive when it enters the world. Babies given this treatment apparently talk a lot earlier than those who haven't been.

  There is a great deal of evidence which indicates that experiences in early childhood are very important, and that the effects are long-lasting. A small child develops 'self-esteem' via the esteem it gets from its parents or parent substitutes. A child who is continually told it has low status is likely to grow into a low-status adult. If you don't experience a quality like compassion as a small child, then it becomes very difficult to develop this quality in adulthood. The incidence of child and sex abuse among people who experienced it themselves as children is horrifyingly high.

- Your own will: the role that 'free will' plays in our psychology is much debated. We know that cause and effect play an important part in the universe, and science shows us how this works. Is personality purely the result of conditioning from parents, the environment and/or society? Or are we able to exert freedom of choice regardless of what is determined by other factors? It's a case of 'determined' (by causes outside our control) versus 'self-determination'. Are you able through your own will to fulfil yourself, to overcome your conditioning?

- The society you live in: some commentators place a high value on our 'social needs' and the extent to which we adapt to live in our society. 'Role theory' says that where we arrive in society shapes our lives. Our goals, values and actions are determined by society. We know what expectations and functions society expects of us, and these give us our status within it. Society's values are passed on to us as children via our families.

- How you regard your 'mind': certain theories, like behaviourism, play down the importance of the human 'mind'. Our responses, it says, are conditioned by reward and punishment from our surrounding environment. We behave in certain ways because the results are useful to us. We don't do things out of choice or purpose but because we are rewarded for what we do. 'Mind' is confined to mechanical functioning of the brain.

Is there such a thing as 'mind'? What is it? Both Freud and Jung considered that we have conscious and unconscious parts to the mind. And they both considered that dreams reflected the workings of the unconscious mind, Freud emphasising how dreams express repressed instincts, Jung investigating symbolism within them. In the 1950s scientific experiment appeared to confirm the existence of an 'unconscious', or at least a part of the brain where all experiences were stored. Dr Wilder Penfield discovered that, by touching a specific part of the brain with a mild electric current passed through a probe, he could reactivate memories and responses to these events in his patients. The patients were under only local anaesthetic, and so were conscious at the time and able to talk to the doctor. The memories they described in response to the stimulus were highly specific and no longer consciously recollected; on experiencing the memory they also relived the feelings they had at the time. To many people the idea of a controlling unconscious mind is a threatening one, which explains to some extent the suspicions directed towards psychoanalysis.

From the angle of this book the views of Alfred Adler are significant. It has been pointed out (by Anthony Storr and Joel Kovel: see Reading List) that Adler's influence has been considerable but under-rated. A contemporary of Freud, he differed from the master over his emphasis on sexuality as the most important motivation on personality. He defected from Freud's psychoanalytic school and insisted that we were mainly motivated by 'strivings for superiority'. He later described this instinct as a 'striving for perfection' and an 'upward striving'. He believed that we all have an 'inborn social feeling' and an 'inescapable characteristic of empathy'. As children, he thought, because of our dependency on adults and physical vulnerability, we all get to experience inferiority. Our self-esteem is dependent on their responses to us.

Adler paid less attention to the unconscious mind and more to goal-directed therapy. His thinking has affected modern approaches to therapy and to counselling and education. Indeed, in some of his pronouncements Adler seems to have been ahead of his time. Rather like today's optimistic prophets on the 'new age', he foresaw 'an ideal society yet to be developed, which comprises all men; all filled by the common striving for perfection'.

FOR OPTIMISTS ONLY

In some ways it may be considered that psychology has gone too far. People are let off heinous crimes because of a 'psychological' explanation. Murderers, rapists and muggers are innocent victims of society, their parents and traumatic early experience. As such they don't deserve punishment, rather understanding and sympathy. It's not their fault. 'Psychobabble' can let them off the hook.

Anyone who studies psychology must be motivated by a streak of optimism that people have the potential to change. Whether they believe that we change through investigation of the unconscious mind, through investigation of the relationship that forms between a therapist and client, through group experience or through changing patterns of behaviour will depend to some extent on which one of these experiences they can best identify with themselves. It seems to me that anyone attracted to practising psychology or psychotherapy or psychiatry has not been so without some needs of their own. Understanding brings enlightenment.

If you are attracted to knowing more about your own psychology (and other people's), or have low self-esteem or emotional problems and would like to do something about it, then you need to decide how 'deep' you want to go. Here's a quick consumers' guide:

- You may just want to dip into the subject via books. In which case, *Life and How to Survive It* by Robin Skynner and John Cleese is a good starting point, as are Dorothy Rowe's books. Anthony Storr is also very readable. Many of the older personality theorists have also written extensively on their ideas. See the Reading List for further suggestions.

- At the deepest level, if you want to explore your unconscious mind be prepared to spend time and money. Psychoanalysts themselves undergo five sessions of analysis a week for five years or so before they can practise. You're likely to need to attend on a regular basis for a couple of years. Don't expect a smooth ride; liberating that which is repressed can be quite traumatic. The process can be painstakingly slow and the results difficult to predict and measure. You may expect direction and advice which will not be forthcoming. The most you may be able to say at the end of it is that you 'gained understanding'; to some of us that may be unsatisfactorily intangible, while to others it may be of profound significance. The schools of Freud and Jung are now much closer together than they used to be: it's been said that Jungians tend to be more 'spiritually' orientated. Read *A Complete Guide to Therapy* by Joel Kovel before you choose.

There are many critics of psychoanalysis. It's argued that psychoanalysts are motivated by the need to influence and control. It's a good way of getting status. *Against Therapy* by Jeffrey Masson argues this point.

- In the last couple of decades what's been called the 'human potential' movement has gathered impetus. This umbrella term covers a large number of different therapies, which concentrate strongly on the 'wholeness' of a person and their potential for good. Carl Rodgers, who has written in a clear, direct way about his experiences, is the strongest influence and in some ways a direct descendant of Alfred Adler. He places strong emphasis on empathy and optimism and less on the need to investigate the unconscious mind. His theories are used in one-to-one therapy, group therapy, training and organisations. On the whole the 'human potential' therapies require less of a time-and-attendance commitment than psychoanalysis, and there are more opportunities for group workshops.

- Group therapy can be particularly suitable for 'problem' families, marital difficulties and as support for addiction or living with addiction. Counselling can help all sorts of crises and the reactions they cause. But be aware that anyone can call themselves a 'counsellor'; your doctor may be able to refer you appropriately – otherwise shop around and go on recommendation.

- One theory suggests that personality can be viewed as a series of concentric rings. At the centre, deep down, we have 'core personality', highly resistant to change, and a part that is perhaps

15

reached most effectively through psychoanalysis. One layer out from the core, made up of thoughts and feelings, we have our self-image – who we believe ourselves to be. The final, outer, layer is our behaviour, our personality as perceived by others. This outer layer is the most receptive and adaptable to change. The remainder of this chapter concerns itself with these two outer layers.

A final point in this section. Some people have the view that it's self-indulgent or self-centred to seek help for difficulties. We should be self-sufficient, or our families or religious beliefs should provide answers. But the traditional family and the influence of religion are in decline in Britain – indeed, the influences of family and religion may be contributing substantially to our difficulties. Not believing in reincarnation or the after-life, it's my view that our lives are not dress rehearsals. We are able, if we choose, to make the most of them. To do that there may be times when we need to put trust in a professional to help solve our difficulties. We need help to go some way towards knowing ourselves and in turn to be able to understand and help others.

LOW-POWER LABELS

As power is a relative quality, for many of us, our conscious awareness of labelling ourselves 'low-power' usually depends on the people and the situation. You may feel secure in your role within the family, but a new boss at work, for example, may mean that your assumptions about your professional power are challenged. Secure in your status at work, becoming a parent may cause confusion – a woman may have to adjust from a professional role to a maternal one, where her own needs become relegated; a father may have to adjust to there being a new small person in the family who makes his role seem less significant. Marriage, divorce, a new job, redundancy or sudden success may find questions like 'am I adequate?' or 'do I really deserve this?' rising to the surface.

When we label ourselves 'low-power' the response may cover other messages, which can include:

- '*I cannot change*'
  Human beings are often described as 'creatures of habit'. At its

most extreme 'I cannot change' can describe a sense of complete impotence – 'I am unable to make any difference to my own or anybody else's life.'

We resist change because of fear of the unknown and because change can threaten our fragile sense of identity – when my self-image is indistinct, I must hold on desperately to those parts I can see, so that they survive. Change is threatening when you are not confident of your own resources.

As small children we may not always get the understanding we need from our parents. We have power over our parents in that we cry out for our needs to be met, and our parents may be anxious and confused about how to do this. They may envy us our power and dependency, which, despite appearing to be contradictory qualities, are not. Being human, with their love, they may resent the sense of duty we stir in them.

Our parents search for strict guidelines to help heal their confused feelings towards us. They will recollect the guidelines they were given themselves as children. They will pass these on to us: 'You are exceptionally important', 'Other people matter more than you do', 'If you're a good girl/boy I will love you', 'I will overpower you if you are naughty.' As these guidelines are rigid, unspoken and unquestionable, many of us live our lives without investigating them. We get more and more guidelines demonstrated, acted out and spoken by our parents: 'Don't ask so many questions', 'Little girls should be seen and not heard', 'Little boys don't cry.' These guidelines shape who we are, our beliefs, values and attitudes, and we are understandably terrified of letting them go, whether we react in compliance with them or against them. Without these guidelines, who are we?

As we grow older and closer to the unanswerable questions concerning our own mortality, it's hardly surprising that most of us cling more strongly to that which we know and become set in our ways. We become more resistant to change and often surround ourselves with friends who strongly reinforce our own self-images.

'I cannot change' as contrasted with 'I choose not to change' describes a sense of hopelessness. Hope is about the unknown and prospects, about balancing our needs for security with the dangers of freedom. We can evaluate what those prospects are and, if we choose to, venture forth in search of the unknown.

- *'I will fail'*
  There are pay-offs contained in this message. If we expect failure,
  we needn't take risks. When we are small we learn from our
  parents that risks are dangerous. Risk involves appearing vulnerable, stupid, isolated. Other people may attack, humiliate, avoid
  us. With us all jockeying for position in the status stakes, we
  can't afford for this to happen. No risks taken means no failure
  and no likelihood of looking stupid.

We may become timid because we're avoiding risks. We start to
notice that people look after us and protect us, especially if we're
girls. We start to feel special. We find this role of little victim useful
– nothing need be our fault or responsibility. Our passive exterior
may conceal a ferocious anger at having limited our choices, and we
may direct this anger into manipulating others.

Through our families we get a sense of a collective viewpoint on
society. Life may be regarded as an austere struggle, blighted by
fate, where only the rich and the lucky fare well. That family identity is one of 'losers'. From an early age, you may be conditioned to
have low expectations. If you can't expect much, why bother? Or
life may be regarded as a battlefield fit for conquerors, with rich
pickings for the strong. Yes, born into a family of 'winners' you can
achieve anything. Anything, that is, until you seem to be slow to
talk and read, particularly in contrast with that incredibly bright
elder sister of yours. . . . Your parents describe you to their friends
as 'difficult'. You start to be naughty. This gets a reaction. You
matter now – you're getting attention and recognition. Your
parents 'can't do a thing with you'. Never mind, you have a definition – you are a 'bad child', which is infinitely preferable to not
knowing what sort of child you are at all. You are a rebel with an
identity cause, a spectacular failure.

When some of us are small we hear a great deal of criticism, more
of the negative than the positive. We don't hear a great deal of
praise. Our own powers of evaluation develop and we get an 'inner
critic'. We may have been bombarded by our parents with many
messages like 'You must try harder' and 'You're not getting it right.'
Our parents may want us to have 'what they never had' – may want
us to fulfil their own frustrated dreams. And they may envy our
potential to do this.

Our inner critic starts to become very responsive. Like our
parents, we set high goals for ourselves. Our identity is tied up with

being someone who never achieves these goals. We are constantly criticising ourselves and, according to our high standards, constantly under-achieving. Like our parents, we can never be 'good enough' and failure is inevitable.

We need our inner critic to discriminate and to set goals and standards for ourselves. When it gets out of control, no matter how successful we are in the eyes of other people, in our heads that critical voice will tell us that we have failed. We are unable to love ourselves enough to allow for weakness. All 'successful' people have earned that description via their ability to cope with failure

- '*I'm addicted to guilt*'
  We experience guilt when we blame ourselves or our actions for events. So guilt is to do with taking responsibility and expecting punishment.

Pride and guilt are closely linked. The greater the sense of pride in who we are and what we do, the more we feel we deserve reward and praise. And when we fail to live up to our own high expectations, the more we feel we deserve punishment and blame. Some of us disown these qualities on a conscious level, and project them on to someone else. When we feel guilty we make other people feel that way as a denial of our own sense of pain. We may even do this through becoming ill, working ourselves into the ground or suppressing our own needs in order to care for others. We become martyrs to make others feel guilty. Guilt is an extremely powerful currency, in which many of us trade.

Bereavement is often accompanied by strong guilt feelings. We deserve to be punished because we considered ourselves over and above the deceased. It's somehow all our fault and we deserve punishment. As small children, when we start to become critical and evaluative we start to challenge our parents. We go into battle with them and they win. They may threaten us in order to control us. They are right and we are wrong. We have to believe they are right because they have played such an important part in our identity and in defining the world for us. If they are wrong, then we are without guidance and they may leave us, which would be catastrophic. In their 'rightness' they leave us with a profound sense of 'wrongness' which many of us store to considerable effect, decades later. When we consider this dilemma for the child between 'rightness' and 'wrongness' and wanting to be loved, we can start to

19

understand the traumatic guilt experienced by victims of child abuse.

Guilt is about 'shoulds' and 'should nots'. It can be helpful to ask yourself, when plagued with conscious guilt, whether you *want* to do something, rather than telling yourself that you should. Is the punishment that you fear really likely? Guilt can also lead us to put a brave face on everything while we overload ourselves with responsibilities and goals. Unrealistically high expectations ensure that we maintain our addiction and keep our guilt levels high.

When we are defined early on in our lives as bad and worthless we may become addicted to guilt. It confirms and reasserts our identity.

- *'I'm in awe of authority'*
  In the early 1960s Stanley Milgram, a research psychologist at Yale University, carried out a series of experiments on the extent to which we obey authority. He got a group of people to administer electric shocks to a group of victims in the belief that they were taking part in an experiment to study the effect of punishment on learning. No shock was actually administered. Different levers raised the voltage of the 'shocks' and the whole experiment was supervised by an authority figure in a white coat, who informed the 'torturers' that they should continue even if they flagged. The 'torturers' were assured that the 'shocks', though extremely painful, would cause no permanent damage.

Though many of the 'torturers' became extremely stressed during the experiment, all of them raised the voltage to levels marked 'very strong' – over 300 volts. At this level the 'victim' was to be heard pounding on the wall. Twenty-six out of 40 of the 'torturers' went up to the 450-volt level. Psychologists had predicted that only just over one in a thousand people would go this far. When the experiment was carried out using phone instructions however, only nine out of a group of 40 obeyed totally. Others lied. It would seem that we are far more likely to obey unquestioningly when the authority figure is actually present.

The more power you give to a large number of authority figures, the more, relatively, you diminish your own. As children, we are all vulnerable to the abuse of authority by parents. As we get older, we may be abused by other authority figures – teachers, doctors, bosses. Authority figures who abuse their power are, of course, doing so because they have received that sort of abuse themselves (and in

20

receiving have also learned how to give abuse) and perhaps because they perceive others as a threat: 'I will dominate you before you have any chance of dominating me.' Chapter Six considers ways of dealing with people who wield authority in this way.

In allowing authority figures to wield power over us indiscriminately, we surrender our rights to choose to take responsibility. Some people might argue that responsibility restricts freedom: they are ignoring our needs to be dependent on others and to have others dependent on us – our sense of belonging. This involves giving others responsibility for your welfare, and in turn taking responsibility for theirs. At worst, it lets someone else do your thinking for you. We will avoid confrontation because of this awe of authority.

- '*I will be rejected by others*'
  Raising your status means that you become more prominent. Others may envy your power. They may reject you and isolate you because you are different from them and they would like to be like you. You may become lonely.

As we grow up we model ourselves on our parents, identifying with them and imitating them. We also fight to separate ourselves from them, to establish a degree of self-sufficiency. If we don't succeed in this then we may require other people to act as our parents, or we may regard others as a threat to this self-sufficiency and therefore avoid intimacy. We may shun involvement with other people because it threatens our identity, and so we remain aloof. We may constantly try to assert our individuality and separateness from others by inevitable disagreement, rejection of their views and immediate aggression towards them so that we stage pre-emptive strikes. We may construct defences for our sensibility by being deliberately offensive, diminishing others and not listening to them.

We may look to others for approval and definition. When other people criticise or praise us we pay a great deal of attention to those descriptions and whether they are true or not, start to act them out. The opinions of others may direct us how to think and react. We may expect other people to fear rejection in the same way that we do, and be surprised by their directness. We may not be able to say no to those people ourselves, because we imagine that they are as susceptible and sensitive to rejection as we are. Other people may take advantage of the sense they get that we are desperate for approval. Our desire to please them will take precedence over our own needs, and our self-possession will be compromised.

All of us need approval unless we choose to live in complete isolation from other people. When we give others the power to define us, we surrender our status. We may project the values we use ourselves on to other people – imagining that they are as critical as we are. We may criticise them, using our own high expectations, and find that they fall short. We may appear superior to them in adopting this thinking. We will also, of course, imagine that they have high expectations of us. In the search for approval, praise is everything, and when others omit to praise us we interpret this as rejection.

When we allow ourselves to be dominated by the demands and opinions of others, our own self-esteem diminishes. We start to resent the power these people have over us. We get envious of them, and constantly compare ourselves to them. We are never good enough. Insecure about our own power, we resent theirs.

The stereotypical role-playing that we see in our families and society may affect our fear of rejection. When your most familiar role models are those of a compliant woman or the 'strong, silent type' of man you may find it difficult to reconcile these influences with the aggressive determination you feel as a female, or the sensitivity and intuition you experience as a man.

INCREASING YOUR POWER

There is no quick, easy, universal solution to low self-esteem – would that there were. If the problem becomes acute – that is, you feel inadequate most of the time – then it is best to seek professional advice. The following list of suggestions contains exercises which are used on management development courses that I'm involved in running with other trainers. These courses are run over several months, giving participants time to try out the suggestions over a period of time. Which ones work most effectively depends on the individual. We have had reports from a high percentage of attendees that their levels of self-esteem and confidence have increased considerably. We have to balance this response with a consideration of the relationship the participants develop with the trainers, and to put some of the enthusiastic response down to a desire to please us and to peer group pressure. Reports of efficacy also need to be tempered with the proviso that building self-esteem is a task which requires constant vigilance against old negative messages.

Here are some approaches to building self-esteem:

Setting Time Aside

The first commitment to be made needs to be one of time. Even if it's just ten minutes a day, allocate some time for your self-esteem programme. It may just be a question of getting up ten minutes earlier in the morning or taking ten minutes when you get in from work to be alone and to reflect and relax.

Self-assessment

Building self-esteem is about appreciating strengths and developing them as much as it is about gaining an understanding of weaknesses. Psychologists use personal construct theory to get people to determine their own values and beliefs. The following exercises can help you identify the criteria you use for assessing others, and in turn how you use them on yourself:

- *Determining values*
  Jot down on a piece of paper the names of three people whom you are close to. Write down their good points and where they could improve. Regard this as your opportunity to play God, and do it fairly quickly. Compare the people with one another and identify what they have in common, and what you approve and disapprove of. For instance:

  Person A: loyal, self-opinionated, good sense of humour, outgoing, sociable, generous, self-disciplined, assertive
  should be: better informed, less ready to champion causes indiscriminately, less obsessive

  Person B: loyal, emotional, charming, self-disciplined, witty, dynamic, energetic, impulsive
  should be: more analytical and self-directing, less ready to please people, less sensitive to criticism

23

Person C: cynical, expresses views strongly, good raconteur, humorous, careful with money, bookish, pays lots of attention to detail
should be: more sensitive to others, more generous with self and others, prepared to take more risks

A is more assertive than B and C, and won't listen to other views.
B is the keenest to be liked, socially most adept, but easy to dominate.
C is the most intellectual and best informed, less impulsive than A and B, but very resistant to change.

From the above, we can extract that the person doing the exercise values strong opinions, sociability, humour, assertiveness, charm, loyalty to people, thoroughness, self-discipline and intellect as strengths; and sees loyalty to causes, lack of information and analysis, over-anxiety to please people, caution, lack of sensitivity, meanness and inflexibility as weaknesses.

From this the person can learn a lot about how they see themselves. Much of what is approved of may match up in their self-image with how they see their strengths and qualities of which they would like more. The qualities that are disapproved of are ones they don't think they have, or consider that they keep under control. Omissions in values, too, are significant. In the above example no mention is made of success, authority, compassion, ability to make money, toughness, talent or hard work. These values, then, are not so important in how the person assesses themselves or others.

- *Life map*
  This exercise is a review of your life so far. On a piece of paper draw a line or pictures, or allocate areas of the page, to mark significant events in your life as far back as you can recall. At each significant event determine whether you were

  (a) powerful or powerless
  (b) comfortable or uncomfortable
  (c) controlled by others or controlling others.

  Does a significant pattern emerge?

- *Positive perspective*
  List your strengths and weaknesses in two columns. It can help to divide the list up into sections – your personality, how you func-

tion at work, how you deal with relationships. Then add other people's views – choose a member of your family, a friend and someone you work with. Recall praise and criticism you've been given. Be as specific as you can. If the weaknesses column is overloaded, try and be a little kinder on yourself. Take your weaknesses and translate them into positives. For instance, 'judgemental about people' can translate into 'highly discriminating'. Here are some other translations that may prove helpful:

dour – realistic	rude – direct
ruthless – single-minded	compliant – agreeable
lazy – relaxed	hypocritical – adaptable
forgetful – creative	guilty – conscientious
aggressive – dynamic	pernickety – thorough.

This exercise shows that the way in which we view the world is completely a question of how we see things and where we're coming from. This can be a helpful approach in discussion – someone may regard you as stubborn, whereas you see yourself as determined. When you're criticised by others, there can be great solace in thinking quietly to yourself about the flip side of the description. (For more on criticism see Chapter Six.)

RETRAINING YOUR CRITIC

Your inner critic can become a useful friend. As the triggers that motivate us may change according to circumstance, the ability to listen to your inner voice and let it direct you is a useful one. We often ignore intuition, when it's possible that intuitive responses are our past experiences lodged in our unconscious minds. Many of us place more value on action, decisiveness and 'pulling ourselves together' than we do on contemplation and reflection in solitude. Quiet introspection can be extremely valuable, especially for people who lead busy, hectic lives and spend little time alone. You can't trust your inner resources if you don't know them. Some people find meditation and yoga useful for these purposes.

Examine the conditioning affecting your critic voice. Does it have your achievements on record as well as your failures? Is your critic in the present? Some of us dwell too much on failure in the past, or the threat of disaster in the future, sending messages like 'You did this very badly last year' or 'Things are bound to go well in the future'. These messages are often to do with guilt: 'I don't deserve things to go well for me.' They can become self-fulfilling prophecies: you go into a situation expecting to fail, even wanting to if it reinforces your self-image – and the inevitable happens. It's sometimes worth asking that nagging little voice what is really the worst thing that can happen *now*?

To re-educate your critic takes time. One useful formula is to assess your performance in terms of

(a) what went well, how did I utilise my strengths and what results did they produce?
(b) what did I learn?
(c) what went badly, and what beneficial feedback does that give me for the future?

If you suspect your inner critic is being accurate in an attack, ask yourself what you can do to make amends. Compensate in a way that is proportional to the 'crime'. Ask yourself how you would respond if you were the 'victim', and what form of compensation would be appropriate. Assess the 'crime' without beating yourself up with knowledge of your past bad record.

Tackle some of your critics' repeated messages by doing the following exercise:

● *Should and can choose*
Put down on paper some of your critic's messages, making them as specific as possible. For instance: 'You should lose weight', 'You shouldn't be so inarticulate at work', 'You shouldn't pursue money as a goal', 'You should be kinder to your mother when she phones for a long chat.' Then look at those messages and ask yourself who in your life is supporting them. What's in it for them in doing this? Then evaluate realistically the outcome if you choose to follow the message, and the outcome if you choose not to follow the message, under a 'can choose' column. For example it might read:

Message: Shoulds	Can Choose
You should lose weight: wear nicer clothes, feel better?	Wear same clothes (supported by husband – pay-off for him – you feel less secure about him so work harder to please him)

Message: Shoulds	Can Choose
You shouldn't be so inarticulate: impress superiors at work	Image the same (supported by boss – pay-off for her – you're less of a threat to her)
You shouldn't pursue money as a goal: tangible rewards for effort, better lifestyle	Try and find other goals?, financial worries (supported by friend – pay-off for him – you don't make me feel inadequate if we're earning the same)
You should be kinder to your mother: less moaning and martyrdom from her	Moaning continues (supported by your mother – you give me attention if I make you feel guilty)

In many cases, the repercussions of not choosing to follow the message are not that extreme. The pressure that the message exerts, by comparison, is considerable. Say 'So what?' to some of these messages, and see what happens. Directing your critic towards the specific is most useful. Get it to analyse specific behaviour and situations rather than to censure you as a person. It's the difference between 'That presentation did not go well, because you mumbled' and 'You made a complete prat of yourself in there.'

Some people find positive visualisation and affirmation helpful. Rather than setting unrealistically high expectations that you then fail to realise, or low expectations that become a self-fulfilling prophecy, take time out to sit and visualise a situation going well. Affirmations are positive statements that you repeat regularly to yourself – for instance to help you with self-esteem. So if you're on a diet, rather than focussing on deprivation you tell yourself, 'Every day I'm getting fitter and healthier.' Or if you feel unappreciated by others, 'I am loved and of value to others.'

Many people say these methods work well – I'm not sure whether they effectively counter strong negative messages from early years. As for affirmations, well, when slogging away to meet a deadline I've found that repeating, 'You're tougher than you think' while gulping down a large glass of gin works a treat.

GOING FOR GOALS

We need challenges in life, and excitement. One of the biggest causes of dissatisfaction at work is insufficient challenge and stimulus, or underload. Some of us may compensate for this by driving our cars like dervishes or creating dramas in our personal lives. Goals need to be realistic, flexible and worked out, and should include both short- and long-term plans. You need to give yourself incentives and rewards, as well as receiving them from other people.

- On a sheet of paper, write down what you want and need professionally, personally, and in material and emotional terms. Then assess your resources:

    (a) what information and knowledge do you have or can you get?
    (b) what skills do you have that can be utilised?
    (c) who can help you?
    (d) what thoughts and feelings do you have towards these goals?
    (e) what's in your way?

Where there are gaps in matching up goals to resources, what can you do about it? Where can you get advice? One of the best resources you can use is a good listener who will allow you to verbalise your doubts and fears aloud and who is capable of listening to you without pressing home their own agenda. You can make this a reciprocal arrangement.

Insufficient challenge is very demotivating. Sometimes it's necessary to leap in and find yourself doing something without procrastination. Waiting to get motivated may be a way of avoiding fear of failure. Work out the pros and cons of what you are considering, and if your instinct is telling you to give it a try then go ahead. If you need to research or get further information, check that this is vital and that you're not using this as an excuse. Is there anything practical you can do immediately? Confront your fears by asking yourself what practical steps you would be taking if you were feeling motivated – make a list and do them. Deep fears can be helped by tackling smaller, more immediate, ones, and the rewards of gradual progress encourage us to continue.

CHANGING DIRECTION

Low self-esteem can be exacerbated by a sense of being a square peg in a round hole. Many of the important decisions we take in life – whom to marry, what career to follow – are taken when most of us are too young and have too little experience really to 'know ourselves'. Marriage guidance counselling can help you to examine the history of your relationship. Professional career counsellors can assess your strengths and weaknesses and offer advice.

We may be hanging on to relationships which reinforce low levels of self-esteem. We may need to confront this situation and realise that we can get greater support from people who have similar motivation to our own.

New skills can increase personal satisfaction. Women in particular are susceptible to believing that improving their appearance can help them reinvent themselves. This is unrealistic, but outward appearances do indicate to others how much we value ourselves. Physical well-being can help create confidence.

Finally, I want to mention two approaches to developing self-awareness and increasing self-esteem: transactional analysis and assertiveness training. I mention them briefly because among management trainers they have many aficionados; they are written about more fully elsewhere. (See the Reading List for details.)

Transactional Analysis

This divides the personality into three parts: parent, adult and child. These divisions establish themselves in the first five years or so of our lives.

- The parent is the last to develop; this is the part of the personality that looks after us. It divides into the critical parent, the judgemental voice in our heads, giving us instructions and punishment, how to behave and what we should do; and the nurturing parent who cares for us, and meets our needs, supports, helps and educates.

- The adult is the rational, logical part of the personality. It works out problems, makes decisions and estimates pros and cons. The adult is concerned with thinking and objectivity. When people experience low self-esteem, their 'adult' may not be as active as it could be.

- The child is the dependent part of the personality, the part that appears earliest. Like the parent, it divides into two. The free child is the part that feels, wants, needs and expresses intuition, emotion and creativity. The adapted child is the part that has learnt how to adapt and fit in with other people – it learns how to please and get approval, and how to manipulate and submit.

Quite clearly, then, if a child is brought up so that it is exposed constantly to a critical parent, she or he may spend much of the time being an adapted child. In other words, if you are brought up on a diet of do's, don'ts, should's and shouldn'ts, you will be inclined to spend a lot of time and energy earning approval.

We can use transactional analysis to identify, through their behaviour, what state people are using. Clearly, if I speak from my critical parent state too often, patronising you and moralising at you, directing you as a child, and you retaliate in a parent state and attempt to direct me back as a child, we've got a 'crossed transaction'. This is when misunderstandings arise. Transactional analysis can be a useful tool in understanding problems with communication in relationships.

Assertiveness Training

Assertiveness skills start from a basic premise – that we all have certain rights. The bill of rights reads like this. We all have the right:

- To be treated with respect.

- To have and express feelings and opinions.

- To be listened to and taken seriously.

- To set our own priorities.

- To say no without feeling guilty.

- To ask for what we want.

- To ask for information from others.

- To make mistakes and to be wrong.

- To choose not to assert ourselves.

- To let our needs be as important as those of others.

Assertive behaviour is characterised by respect for your own rights and needs, and for those of other people. The status of both parties remains intact. *Aggressive behaviour* is defined as coming from a belief that your rights are more important than other people's, and that in seeking to meet your needs you can violate those of others. You attack other people's status. *Submissive behaviour* is defined as coming from a belief that your rights and needs are less important than other people's and that others can violate them. Your status is diminished. Behaviour styles match these definitions.

Here are some basic assertiveness techniques:

- *Three-part messages*:
  This formula can help you express messages that make you feel uncomfortable. It goes:

  describe
  disclose
  predict

Use simple, direct language and be as specific as possible. Like this:

  describe: when you don't take down messages/call me back/ encourage me.
  disclose: I feel: irritated/like I don't matter/defeated.
  predict: if you do this, I can work more efficiently/I know you're busy, but if you do this we'll both save time on discussions like this/I'd be better motivated if you did.

- *Broken record*:
  Calm repetition. Very useful. For instance:

  Anne: I need some time off next week. Do you think I could take Monday off, please?
  Bill: Take the call for me, would you?
  Anne: As I was saying, I need some time off next week. . . .
  Bill: Not now, Anne. I'm up to my eyes in it here. Can we talk later?
  Anne: I'd like to get this settled now. I need some time off –
  Bill: Yes, I heard you. Next week – all right, Monday afternoon it is. Now can I get on, please?

It's clear that behaviour style needs to be appropriate to assertiveness. Irritated and aggressive behaviour can cause conflict.

- Fielding and fogging
  In the above example Anne hears what Bill says, but doesn't allow herself to get deflected from her purpose. She 'fields' what he says.

Fogging is to do with acknowledging the other person's viewpoint and then continuing with your purpose. For instance, 'I know you're terribly pushed, but can I ask you quickly. . . .'

The importance of behaviour matching up to assertive messages cannot be over-emphasised. There will be further examples of assertiveness in the following chapter, showing how techniques can be used to influence. Chapter Six contains further mention of its application in dealing with high-power people and conflict. The final chapter shows how to match your behaviour to high-power messages.

chapter two

POWER OF
INFLUENCE

Power is always about who does the defining and who accepts
the definitions.

Dorothy Rowe, *Beyond Fear*

You can use your personal power to gain recognition from
others. Defined in the dictionary as 'ability to do or act',
'power' has numerous connotations. We 'power dressed' in
the 1980s, we talk of shifts in world power, people are described
as having 'powerful presence'. The way in which we regard, seek
and use power shapes our relationships, our ambitions and our
successes.

Power is a redundant resource unless it is used, and influence is
the use of power. Sometimes, influential people are not the most
overtly powerful. They can be the 'power behind the throne', using
what power they have to its fullest potential: analysing situations,
forming appropriate alliances and putting messages over in a palat-
able way to the right audience. This chapter examines different
ways of exercising power. It gives practical suggestions on how to
develop your influencing skills, on how to become more versatile
when influencing and on how to choose what tactics are best for the
situation. The skills described have widespread application – they
could be used to improve communication at home, to raise money
for a charitable cause or to negotiate with another company over a
takeover bid, for example.

Although this chapter is concerned with how you as an individual
use power, it is worth considering that the global perspective on

power is starting to change. A country's power can be measured by its military and economic resources and the signing of arms agreements; and growth in market, rather than government, control of economies suggest that the way in which these resources are being used is changing. For individuals there is increasing emphasis on freedom of choice.

How do people get power? Why do some of us shy away from it and regard it as 'bad'? Power gives us the ability to control, to choose and to assert our independence. It can be used to positive or negative effect on others. We can get power through:

- *Knowledge and skills*: information power and expert power count for a great deal in the workplace. Professional power depends on these. The quality and amount of information you have about a subject can mark you out as a specialist who is an invaluable source of advice for others. Your information could be to do with other people: knowing what their capabilities are, what motivates them, where they have influence. Expert skills may be related to the tangible, like bookbinding or open-heart surgery, or the more intangible, like negotiation or ability to analyse. Knowledge and skills are a valuable source of power that we can build on and develop.

- *Using the carrot and the stick*: we can get power through our ability to reward and punish others, to give them something or to take it away. When we are children we first experience this use of power by our parents. If you would like a business to help you with a charity appeal, the 'carrot' of good publicity may get them to do so. The 'stick' of going to a rival company who would use the publicity can act as another pressure. The carrot and stick approach is to do with reward and punishment, incentives and pressures.

- *Physical attributes*: some people use their bodies to get power. The body builder, wrestler, aerobics queen and Madonna use their bodies to control the responses of others: to arouse feelings of fear, jealousy, admiration and desire in others. Physical skills and attractiveness are much admired in our society.

  The way in which we clothe our bodies and accentuate our physical attributes can also build power. When we power dressed we made our bodies look angular and more aggressive, with hard, sharp lines. As a source of power, physical attributes may be short-lived and superficial. Some of us think the power they give us is worth clinging on to through plastic surgery

- *Money*: can help us achieve things, influence others, and free us of dependency on people or situations. Like power, money as it stands is neither a good nor a bad commodity. It's how it's used and what people do to get it that can offend our values. Economic independence can create choices and build your self-respect. Some of us suffer from an aversion to talking about money – known as remuneraphobia. We've been brought up to think that it's not nice and not polite to do so. We may accept lower terms than we want for a job or a project, and in undervaluing ourselves we become less powerful in the eyes of others.

- *Title*: this is positional power. We are given a title which carries with it a job or role description that allows us to control and manage others. Title power is overt, as opposed to active, status. A title may reflect little of the holder's active status: in some countries the title 'President' is largely to do with nominal power. Some companies farm out elderly executives to a convenient backwater where they are given a lofty title – Senior Vice President in Charge of Something Unimportant. Forward-thinking organisations have restructured themselves so that adherence to strict hierarchy and title is less significant. We have reverence for titles instilled in us when we are small: many of us have a slightly different response to a 'Dr' than we do to a 'Ms', 'Mrs' or 'Mr'.

- *Personality and behaviour*: this is to do with abstract qualities like 'charisma', 'presence' and 'leadership ability'. Power that comes from who you are and how you represent yourself and behave towards others is highly contagious. Other people will admire you and aspire to be like you. You may act as a role model and a mentor to others.

  Personal power is about knowing and valuing yourself, and trusting your inner resources. It's about accepting and dealing with responsibility and not being overwhelmed by it. It's to do with having a balanced overview of your strengths and weaknesses and not using these to the detriment of others or so that others are able to exploit you. You are able to define, to make sense of people and situations while listening to others who help you with this definition. Self-assured enough to make decisions, clarify your goals and take risks, other people's definitions, needs and opinions do not represent a threat to you.

Sounds too good to be true? It probably is. It's a description to aspire to. Very few of us remain confident of our personal power in every situation and with every sort of person. When we are insecure about our personal power, ill at ease with our individuality and allowing others to define us much of the time, we may rely heavily on other sources of power. For instance we can tend to:

- Constantly air our knowledge to others, and bore them about our skills.

- Promise carrots we can't deliver, or use threats that are destructive and cruel.

- Use money to buy friends and assert superiority.

- Use physical attributes to intimidate and seduce others.

- Use our titles and authority position, rather than our own skills, to get what we want.

We can learn to develop our personal power through identifying the resistance we have to using certain types of behaviour and learning skills that make us more adaptable. Influence is to do with 'non-material' power and is not tied to positional power or title – though having this resource may offer greater opportunities for influence. The Mother Teresas, Bob Geldofs and Martin Luther Kings of this world have had considerably more influence than the Gerald Fords and the Imelda Marcoses.

POO-POOHING POWER

We have all known powerlessness. As babies we relied on others for food, shelter, protection and love. We were defined by other people – our parents or parent figures. We were dependent and scared when we thought the powerful people had left us, were not attending to our needs, or were angry and cruel to us. We were confused and anxious when we were not understood.

When we hear the word 'power' some of us make strong associations with fear, deprivation and a loss of control. If other people have it they represent a threat to our independence, to our ability to make choices and to our sense of having control over people and situations in our own lives. We must be reactive rather than proactive, because becoming motivated and taking initiatives involves gaining power. We cannot see that power is a means of dealing with fear, of acting and doing in order to gain control over it; when we are powerless our fears overwhelm us.

We think that power is a limited resource, and if one person has it then another one can't. We cannot see that power can be held in different ways, and that personal and professional relationships that work effectively are often a delicate balance see-sawing on power shifts. We cannot visualise ourselves becoming more powerful without damaging others. We are envious of others who have power because they represent a threat. We transfer 'I don't deserve it' on to 'They don't deserve it', and may try to make them feel guilty.

Our social conditioning affects how we regard power. We may have been brought up to believe that it was selfish to put our own needs before others. Our early encounters with power may have deterred us from ever wanting to use it in a similar way; having suffered from a cold, distant father or a smothering mother, and inevitably having attributed power to these parents, we may well decide that power is a negative force and not for us. Little girls may be brought up to see power as something exercised mainly by the men in the family, and not a quality that is sought or used much by women. When they grow up, they may feel uncomfortable with their need for power and unsure how to exercise it. Little boys may be brought up in families where they saw their fathers exercising power in a very macho, bluff way. When they grow up they may think that power is about domination of others without regard to their needs, thoughts and feelings.

Personal power is limitless. When we make good use of power we empower others – in the way that wealthy philanthropists may make good use of their money in helping others. We appreciate our rights and value as individuals while respecting those of others.

GAINING INFLUENCE

There are several different approaches that we can use to build influence. The suggestions that follow are based on models that are widely used in management development and leadership training. All models inevitably contain values of what is good and bad, right and wrong. Some of the approaches described below may have wider appeal to your values than others. It is likely that you are already using some of them; others may seem to be more challenging. Try out in a familiar, low-risk situation the suggestions that you find most challenging. It's better to get comfortable with the approach in a situation where you are confident, like a weekly meeting, than suddenly to try and implement it when you are in a more testing situation, like an important sales presentation. You will need time to become confident with the new skills.

These suggestions are not to do with changing your personality, they are concerned with your behaviour. When we learn anything new we go through several stages:

- (a) Unconscious incompetence.

- (b) Conscious incompetence.

- (c) Conscious competence.

- (d) Unconscious competence.

Stages (b) and (c) can feel quite uncomfortable and self-conscious; we imagine that other people are finding our new behaviour strange. What often sounds and feels stilted to us, because we are learning it, will sound quite normal to everyone else. When we are anxious – and we may well be anxious about trying something new – we tend to stick with the familiar and the tried and tested. So if you have got your way some of the time by being aggressive and forceful, when you try a more considerate approach you will feel insecure. If you have influenced others in the past by being enthusiastic and emotional, you may find it uncomfortable to start using logic.

This view could be called cynical, but my experience leads me to believe that in most situations we are preoccupied with ourselves and our own agendas. Other people have to do something pretty dramatic for us to notice. Putting a case more forcefully or asking for greater involvement from others is likely to get attention for your content rather than for your new style.

THE DOORS OF INFLUENCE

We are all familiar with signs on doors saying 'Push', 'Pull' and 'Exit'. These words conveniently describe three different approaches to influencing. The Push approach (sometimes called the 'cold') describes you moving towards the people you want to influence. The Pull approach (sometimes called the 'warm') describes you drawing the people you want to influence towards you. The Exit approach describes getting away from the people you want to influence, even though this departure may be temporary. You will want to switch from one approach to another according to how people react and circumstances change.

Before you try to influence anyone, you want to establish your purpose and your motives. Most of our communication between one another is indirect; we conceal our motives. Unless you have established for yourself what your motives are beforehand, you are unlikely to be able to present them in an attractive light to others.

You will need to pay attention to the first impression you make. If you are attempting to influence people whom you do not know, you must appear to have integrity and credibility. You will need to establish rapport quickly, so that they can trust you. First impressions indicate to others how they should respond and communicate with us. Once decisions are taken, our 'audience' then look for further evidence in what we say and do to confirm that they are right. Chapter Nine deals with this in greater detail.

It can be more difficult to attempt to influence people who know you, because you perceive they have expectations of you. Your knowledge about them and their likely responses gives you power. You may have to work hard to change their conditioned response. Approach them with a positive attitude and a strong sense that change is possible. You could find it useful to comment on past reactions and to ask for a fresh angle: 'When we've talked about having some staff working from home, we've always got bogged down in cost factors regarding the technology needed. Can we start to look at it this time from the benefits to some people in terms of travel and a quiet environment?'

Bear in mind that when the chips are down, we tend to revert to what we feel comfortable with and what we think has worked effectively in the past. In doing so, we confine our influencing ability to certain people and circumstances. The greater our adaptability the wider our sphere of influence.

Push

This strategy can be divided into two approaches, the forceful and the logical.

The Forceful Approach
You already use this approach if you:

- Let others know what you want and need.
- Let others know what you expect from them, and standards for assessment.
- Are comfortable instructing, directing and correcting others.
- Are quick to praise and criticise.
- Voice your opinion frequently.
- Like to bargain for what you want.
- Find it easy to put pressure on others.

This approach will be useful to you if you:

- Don't like talking about yourself.
- Appear indecisive and submissive.
- Go along with others against your true inclinations.
- Can't say no.
- Avoid conflict.
- Compromise too readily.
- You can appear weak and tentative.

This is an assertive approach to influencing. It is a useful technique for people who are over-anxious for approval from others and who worry too much about making others angry or upset. It's also helpful if you tend to have low expectations of yourself and of making demands on others. There are three elements to this approach:

- (a) *Saying what you want and need*
  Some of us avoid using the word I. In this approach you have to. You can't pretend that you haven't got desires and needs. You must identify them and express them, otherwise frustration and anger build up. Give this message to others in a brief, clear way: 'I need to talk to you about office manning'; 'I don't want to go away this weekend'. Don't be tempted to justify these requests or to give reasons for them. Use the 'Broken Record' technique as described on p. 52, repeating your request when you get objections.

- (b) *Describing what you like and don't like*
  Give your view of how you are feeling about the situation – what are the pros and cons. You are expressing your personal responses, and speaking from the heart as much as from the head, so there is no need to try and paint an apparently 'objective' picture with appeal to the intellect. Try 'I'm pleased that the office manning problem is on next week's agenda – I'm worried that it needs more urgent attention' or 'I love it that you've asked me to go away – it's bothering me that I've got to do this report by Monday.' State what pleases you to begin with – if you state the negative first, the other party may never hear the positive as they start to construct defences to your attack. You can't be accused of whingeing and complaining when you make the other person aware that you can see the positive in the situation too.

- (c) *Using the carrot and the stick*
  Some of us don't realise the extent of our 'carrot and stick' power. We don't use it because we haven't realised our resources. To estimate whether you have this power ask yourself: 'What do I have, or can do, that the other person wants and needs? Can I take anything away from them that they want or need in exchange for what I want and need?' You need to control the carrot and the stick, and only use them when you are prepared to put them into action. There's little point in making promises and threats that you are not prepared, when it comes to it, to carry out. And if you rely too heavily on rewards and punishments and use them too often, their effect becomes diminished. You may not be able to think of incentives and pressures that you can use, just because you haven't given sufficient thought to identify what the other person wants and needs and how you can match them. It can be useful to recap on the action you want taken after putting on pressure: 'If I can talk about it today, then I'll be able to get on with the project – if I can't, the project is going to have to be delayed. So I'd like to talk now.' 'If we go away this weekend I'm not going to be relaxed – next weekend I'll be a lot more fun.'

Putting the two examples together:

1 'I'm pleased that the office manning problem is on next week's agenda – I'm worried that it needs more urgent attention.' (b) 'I need to talk to you about it.' (a) 'If I can talk about it today,

then I'll be able to get on with the project – if I can't, the project is going to have to be delayed. So I'd like to talk now.' (c)

2 'I don't want to go away this weekend.' (a) 'I love it that you've asked me – it's bothering me that I've got to do this report by Monday.' (b) 'If we go away this weekend I'm not going to be relaxed – next weekend I'll be a lot more fun.' (c)

Use this formula, and if necessary jot down on paper how you'll use the three stages and practise it aloud, so that you get comfortable with it.

As this approach is a tough, personal, confrontational one it only works when both parties have something to gain or lose. At work, emotional needs are stronger than a lot of people realise; by letting people know that you have them, and identifying theirs, you can gain influence. What you want and need must be viable and realistic. Your level of control needs to be high enough so that your carrot and stick power matters and is taken seriously by others.

And because this is a strong push for influence, it doesn't work with people who are keenly aware of their position above you in a hierarchy, and who need to feel very much that they're the boss. Using it inappropriately with someone who has very strong feelings on a subject may lead you to be regarded as insensitively self-opinionated. Be aware, too, that behaving this assertively may get agreement from people and acquiescence but it may not get dedication and loyalty. People will go along with what you want rather than actively supporting you. For many people it's riskier than the next approach and there is no guarantee of results; but you will certainly have made a powerful impression on others.

The Logical Approach
You already use this approach if you:

- Enjoy making suggestions and proposals.
- Like to persuade others.
- Frequently suggest solutions to problems.
- Relish debate and argument.
- Use logic and reasoning a great deal.

- Challenge cases that you disagree with.
- Think of another angle when people disagree.

This approach will be useful to you if you:

- Feel apprehensive about offering ideas to others.
- Lack confidence in making a case.
- Stay out of debate in meetings and discussions.
- Fail to get your suggestions considered by others.
- Are undermined by others arguing back.
- Don't think you come over as logical and rational.
- Think that your communication could be better structured.

This approach is useful for people who regard themselves as unable to analyse and rationalise. Sometimes this label may come from a sense of being less-educated than other people, or less articulate. It's also useful for improving performance in almost every work situation, as logical persuasion is how most of us communicate at work. It can enable the reluctant and shy to enter into discussion with greater enthusiasm at home or at work. There are two elements to this approach:

- (a) *Proposing*
  That is, putting forward ideas, suggestions or proposals. You need to believe that these are sound, even if other people don't like them. You should present them with a sense of commitment. They should be relevant to what's going on, so to use this approach efficiently it's important to listen to others. In group meetings, if you tend to be hesitant then get in early with your proposal. As in the previous push approach, it pays to be concise. For instance: 'I think we should be getting some of our employees to work from home' or 'I'd like to suggest that we go home early.' Immediately after the proposal give the . . .

- (b) *Reasoning*
  This is your back-up evidence designed to appeal to people's intellects. It's Push approach to the head, rather than to the heart. Structure, precision and control are all characteristics of logical influencing. For that reason, it's better to stick to a small number of clearly expressed reasons. Reasons are often better thought up beforehand, and this is an approach that benefits particularly from pre-planning. If you tend to forget back-up reasons in the surprise of hearing yourself make a proposal or suggestion, then

use a link to remind yourself: 'And there are two reasons for this.'

When we link reasoning to the above proposals this is what we get:

1 'I think we should be getting some of our employees to work from home.' (a) 'A couple of reasons – the technology is now available to do this, and there could be considerable saving to the company in travel expenses and workspace.' (b)

2 'The electrician is coming at eight tomorrow morning and we're going out to dinner late tomorrow night.' (b) I'd like to suggest that we go home early.' (a)

Reasoning can also be used with summarising. 'No one has any more to say on that point, so I suggest we move on to the next one.'

For your suggestions and proposals to be taken seriously, you need to have credibility with the other people involved. Launching into the logical approach when someone has not had time or does not have the information to assess your credibility is unwise.

The logical approach works very well when you have information or expert power. With specialist information, facts, statistics, case histories and examples that others are unaware of, you can make a good case. The approach also works well when alternatives can be considered and rejected through reasoning and facts.

Proposing and reasoning can appeal to our intellectual vanity. When someone suggests something as opposed to insisting on it, we enjoy the fact that our powers of discrimination and judgement are being recognised. That is why the suggestion 'Why don't you try it?' works so well as a selling technique.

However, this approach may not always be the most successful one because it is so familiar to most of us, and in a competitive situation people are able to go on reasoning until the cows come home. If you try to appear logical and reasonable when others suspect that you have strong emotional motives, then the approach will fail. This is a problem-solving style, which works best when strong emotions are not aroused. Commitment to suggestions and proposals may not be as strong when emotions are not engaged. Some of us try to propose and reason when we cannot cope with another person's emotions. There is nothing more galling, if you care passionately about something or are feeling angry or upset, to be told to 'Be reasonable.'

Pull

Pull strategy can be divided up into two approaches, the participative and the inspirational.

The Participative Approach

You already use this approach if you:

- Ask people for opinions and suggestions.
- Notice and respond to other people's concerns.
- Try and bring in people who are isolated.
- Listen carefully to what people say and how they say it.
- Pay attention to views other than your own.
- Actively supply others with helpful information.
- Are open with your thoughts, feelings and intentions.

This approach will be useful to you if you:

- Always try to control and dominate people and situations.
- Talk too much, and not let others have their say.
- Find it difficult to reveal much about yourself.
- Don't notice other people's problems.
- Listen poorly and don't hear others.
- Regard yourself as 'not very good with people'.
- Are regarded by others as 'pushy' or 'a cold fish'.

If you often get nervous about making a fool of yourself, this approach will help. If nervousness prevents you from participating in events, you may feel isolated and mistrusted by others. This approach can also help those people who feel a sense of threat from other people's opinions and so bulldoze them first so that others are prevented from expressing their views. It is useful for those of us who worry that hearing other opinions and listening to other people may weaken our case, or make it difficult for us to concentrate on our own determined agenda. There are three elements to this approach:

- (a) *Involving others*

  This is to do with drawing people into a situation and asking them for their thoughts and feelings. It's a style that revolves around asking questions: open questions requiring some substance in the answer, rather than closed questions requiring one-word answers. Leading questions which direct people how to respond should be avoided. Use, for example, 'How did you think that went?' rather than 'That was a bit of a disaster, don't you think?'

  Involving others means giving them your support and encouragement. It's letting people know that their contribution has been appreciated, that their ideas are valued and that they can have their say, whether others agree with the content or not. For instance, 'Thanks very much for making that suggestion – do you want to say any more about it?'

- (b) *Active listening*

  The psychotherapist Carl Rodgers pioneered a technique called active listening. This demands that the listener gives the speaker their full, undivided attention, and that she or he summarises, paraphrases, clarifies and interprets rather than directing through responses. It's an extremely difficult technique to perfect. We want to rush in and give solutions, or reassurance when dealing with pain and confusion.

  Active listening means paying attention to the tone of voice, body language and facial expression of the speaker in order to understand the thoughts and feelings behind the words. Frieda Fromm-Reichmann, another eminent researcher, used to mirror the energy and attitude of her clients to increase rapport, a technique that proved successful. So when the speaker was talking rapidly with a lot of energy she would listen with obvious interest, excitement and quick responses.

  Using this method, you are recapping and understanding: 'It sounds like you felt it went very well. Do I understand you think we should enter again next year?'

- (c) *Disclosing*

  As this whole approach is to do with openness, its third part is to do with giving people information they need, with expressing your own thoughts and feelings and asking for help and advice when you need it. It's also to do with using your own past experiences to show empathy and understanding when others need it. It means admitting sometimes that you are confused, frightened, angry and guilty. Disclosure requires you to make yourself vulnerable; in having the confidence to do this you become personally powerful and gain trust from others. They know that you are not trying to portray yourself as a know-all, that you have accepted being 'only human'. They are more likely to open up themselves.

Our conditioning can make us very resistant to using disclosure. Those messages like 'Little boys don't cry', 'Keep a stiff upper lip' and 'Maintain a brave face' make it very difficult to describe experiences where we did not feel in control and did not appear invulnerable. If you have difficulty doing this, use your listening to ascertain what emotional response the speaker is feeling; then ask yourself whether you have a relevant emotional experience that you can offer as encouragement to help them express their response. For instance: 'Well, we didn't do at all well last year and I know it was my fault. I didn't do enough planning and preparation. Even so, I was miserable when we were second from last.'

Putting the above three together we get:

Listener: How did you think that went? (a)
Speaker: Not too badly – we came fourth. It was difficult – you know, first time I'd been in charge.
Listener: Well, we didn't do at all well last year and I know it was my fault. I didn't do enough planning and preparation. Even so, I was still miserable when we were second from last (c). How do you feel about this year's showing? (a)
Speaker: There were forty-seven competing, so given our limited experience of the event I think we did quite well. I was very apprehensive – there were very big seas when we started. We really worked well together as a team, though, and I think everyone really relished the experience.
Listener: It sounds like you felt it went very well. Do I understand that you think we should enter again next year? (b)

The value of this approach is often underestimated. It is essential in researching and gathering information, and works very well in conjunction with any of the other approaches. Use the forceful approach to get attention early on, and then move to this one to negotiate and to find out what rewards and pressures you can offer before returning to the forceful approach. 'I need to talk to you about the cleaning. How do you think the system is working out at present?' If the forceful approach backfires, then use the participative one to get you out of trouble and to cool the temperature: 'My request seems to have made you angry. How would you advise me to deal with this problem?'

In discussion, alternate the logical approach with this one. That way you hear other people's views and can prepare argument and reason which take them into consideration. In the approach that follows, the inspirational, you can use the participative approach to find what exactly it is that you've got in common and what it is that turns people on.

This is an essential skill in managing people, because it gets others involved and committed. If you're overseeing work that you're not directly involved in, this approach is invaluable. Whenever you can't do anything alone, use the participative style to gain support. If people can contribute anything, this is the way to encourage them. Whenever there is any exploration involved – of whether people want to buy something, are prepared to donate money, are open to negotiation, or are performing badly at something – participation is a useful tool. When emotions are running high, this approach is the most effective.

The drawbacks of this style used alone are that it can be slow and you have less control over your objective. When everyone is being encouraged to have their say and chipping in, you can only have decision-making by consensus and that takes a lot of time. If you are genuinely hearing others' opinions then you must be open to influence from them, so you might have to adjust your goalposts. The nature of your case must be such that people can feel commitment towards it. There's no point in asking for feelings and responses on something that nobody gives two hoots about.

In direct contrast with the forceful approach, there must be low risk of the person losing anything from getting involved and committed with your suggestions. And in direct contrast again, this approach may bring you long-term loyalty rather than compliance.

The Inspirational Approach
You already use this approach if you:

- Enjoy finding things in common with others.
- Search for areas of agreement in conflict.

- Unite people in a shared cause.
- Convey enthusiasm and optimism to others.
- Get others to see positive opportunities.
- Fix clear goals with expectations of success.
- Motivate others and make them feel confident.

This approach will be useful to you if you:

- Find it difficult to convey enthusiasm.
- Usually have a sceptical attitude.
- Expect things to go wrong a lot of the time.
- Lack a strong sense of direction.
- Would like to build or be part of a team.
- Want to motivate and lead other people.
- Want to build a more positive outlook.

You may not feel comfortable with this style of influencing, because you find you are tentative about expressing enthusiasm and think it might be interpreted as naivety. Cynics – who adopt their attitude as a defence to protect themselves against their hopes being dashed – may ridicule you. This approach is helpful if you have a tendency to compete with others and view them as a threat; it encourages greater understanding between people and appeals to shared aspirations. Aspirations, a sense of how we can realise our potential, give us power and motivation. To use this approach well, you need to have the confidence to be able to predict what could happen, without worrying too much if you're proved wrong and risk appearing vulnerable. There are two elements to this approach:

- (a) *Finding common ground*
  This is to do with finding values, ideas, goals and areas that are of common interest. It's the 'What's in it for all of us?' factor. It's important that we identify what desires and needs we could have in common with one another when using this approach; if we don't know the people concerned very well, or have not considered them in this way, we need to use the participative approach described above. Once we have identified shared interests, we can point out how they will be met. Sometimes common ground is apparent without needing to say anything: when we're influencing others who have the same job as ourselves, or similar type of backgrounds or lifestyles, we already have a great deal in common. To find common ground we have to be ready to dis-

close information about ourselves and to point out shared interests through chit-chat: 'I heard you went to London University. I
was there at UC and finished in 1978. I'd be interested to know
which college you went to.' We like people who remind us of
ourselves, and we understand and trust them since they reinforce
our self-image. There is a sense of us 'all being in this together'.
The language of this approach emphasises this sense – using 'us',
'we' and 'our' rather than 'yours', 'I' and 'my'.

- (b) *Visualising the future*
  In this exciting, optimistic approach it is important to have the
  ability to create pictures of what could happen in the future –
  ideal solutions and potential achievement. We can use our
  imaginations and think creatively to foresee possible outcomes.
  This style uses metaphors, imagery and colourful descriptive
  language. For instance, 'We can imagine the potential we're considering. It's like a dream in which we've been trying to get
  through to people and we've represented this by seeing ourselves
  locked inside our homes, desperately trying to get out. But we
  can't. Now we find these doors are marked "Push", "Pull" and
  "Exit". We know that we can open them, and when we use them
  we go into a world full of exciting possibilities.'

When we inspire, we lead and motivate. When people are lacking
direction we can use the approach to generate enthusiasm, to create
a sense of team spirit, energy and sense of purpose. It's a strong
approach that's useful in selling, presenting and setting up projects.
It shows people what's in it for them.

To use it effectively, we need to be able to establish common
ground and other people need to be open to direction. We need to
be sure that they respect us and trust us. We need to be aware that
this approach has a strong emotional appeal and that using it
involves taking responsibility and guiding these emotions, once
engaged. In the face of opposition, this approach can establish some
areas over which agreement can be reached.

As far as drawbacks to this approach are concerned, enthusiasm
is highly contagious, but people who don't express it themselves
may find it embarrassing. Switch to the logical approach if this is
the case and then return, once you've made an intellectual appeal,
to this more direct, emotional one. Sometimes we can find it difficult to visualise positive outcomes; if this is the case I suggest you

refer to Chapter One, which explains that all qualities can be given an opposite, more positive, interpretation.

When we identify common ground we need to be sure that we are not making assumptions about other people's values and interests. If you are using this style on a group, it's worth thinking about individuals' values and interests and appealing to them. Some of us resent being regarded as 'one of the herd'.

This approach is not always the most effective in getting definite action; though it is most effective at setting people on course and giving them purpose. You may want another approach to get people to sign on the dotted line.

Exit

You already use this approach if you:

- Delay dealing with issues until you are adequately prepared.
- Allow other people time to prepare.
- Stop discussion when you are overloaded.
- Step back from problems and disruption and analyse what's going on.
- Are good at alleviating tension between people.

You will find this approach useful if you:

- Have difficulty distancing yourself from situations.
- Keep going even though you need time to reconsider or reflect.
- Always get involved in conflict.
- Keep working even though you are feeling under par.
- Respond to personal attack by getting angry or upset.

Reluctance to use this strategy can come from a feeling that you don't have a right to control, that you can't call the shots, that you are powerless. It's different from running away; it's a conscious choice to put off dealing with something until conditions are more favourable to yourself and to other people involved.

- *The standing back approach*
  Someone phones you for a price for a project. They catch you on the hop. You don't want to look silly and you're excited at the prospect of the work, so in the heat of the moment you suggest an unrealistically low price. Wouldn't you have been wiser to call them back?

That in essence is the standing back approach. You take time for yourself and others to stop and think. We can use this approach through postponing decisions, meetings and finding solutions until we have all the necessary information and all the right people present. If we want to influence another person and that person is working under enormous stress and is irritated by our request, we can stand back and wait until she or he is more relaxed. In situations where tempers are getting raised, we can stand back and make everyone aware of what is happening and the effect on progress: 'We all seem to be getting very heated about this, and we've come a long way from the main issue. Can we think back to the original complaints about company car allocation?'

Standing back can mean changing the subject to take pressure off yourself or others. It can be useful to refer to something you all have in common, which may restore a feeling of harmony. Humour, too, can be a way of breaking a tense atmosphere. You can stand back in practical terms, too – suggesting a couple of hours' break for people to clear their heads, or that you finish early in order for people to think over proposals and reconvene in the morning.

This approach is useful when you and others can gain through postponement. It's useful when discussions have become heated and lost any sense of structure or direction. If someone is behaving rashly and will later regret it, use this approach. When people are tired and overloaded and cannot think clearly, take a break. If you are being pressurised by someone, use this tactic; it's the 'I'm just looking, thank you' or the 'I'll go away and think about it' response to the pushy salesperson. It's indispensable as a negotiating tool: 'I'll get back to you.'

There are two drawbacks – the first is that this approach is inappropriate if quick decisions have to be made. The second drawback is that if you spend too much time standing back, commenting on what's going on, using humour and changing the subject you may end up disrupting a collective sense of purpose and fail to meet your objective. The greater likelihood is that, when you suggest a practical stand-back of the 'Shall we go to the pub?' variety, you will have given voice to what a lot of other people have been thinking.

Before I stand back from this chapter, a summary. Push, Pull and Exit are ways of looking at exerting influence. If you haven't done so already, you may find it useful to go through the lists of 'You already use this approach if you ...' and 'This approach will be useful if you . . .', ticking which ones you use most. You should get a picture of how you currently influence and where your strengths could be developed. Keep visualising the future, and may the power of influence be with you. . . .

Chapter three

THE TACTICS OF
TALK

Power signals are constantly being exchanged between us
through what we see and hear. Newspapers are full of messages
that appeal to our concepts of power: profiles of powerful
people in the qualities and 'how the mighty are fallen'-type stories in
the tabloids.

In the late 1980s, scandal rocked the City of London, when three of
its luminaries, Gerald Ronson, Ernest Saunders and Anthony Parnes,
were jailed for insider trading in a takeover bid by Guinness. The case
aroused a great deal of comment. When we hear of dramatic changes in
the defendants' status, from City supremos to detainees of Her Maj-
esty, our reactions are determined by our notions of power. If they
deserved what they got, then they had too much. If they didn't, then
their power was not sufficiently acknowledged. If they should have
been given even more 'porridge', then their belief that their own power
made them beyond the rule of law was insufficiently punished. Whatever the viewpoint, we react in terms of status.

Celebrities and politicians vie for prime-time television and radio
airtime in order to gain influence. And as radio and television are
largely concerned with talk, these aspirants have to be able to do it
to succeed in their quest. On the airwaves the talk is packaged to
appeal to and persuade the mass market – a topic that will be dealt
with later.

Talk is of enormous relevance in understanding power and in
developing your own powers of influence. Every time you meet
someone, they give you rank and recognition according to what you
say and how you say it. You in turn will do the same to them. Both

parties will give rank and recognition according to individual beliefs and values. The 'people like us' factor will ensure that, the greater the compatibility between what you are *apparently* conveying in your talk and what the other person values, the better the outcome.

Many conversations are tussles for power. Unproductive meetings, domestic rows and uncomfortable social chit-chat can all be caused by status needs being ignored and camouflaged. Misunderstandings arise because of what's been said and the way in which it's been interpreted. As participants, we often do not understand what is going on in the interchange, so caught up are we with our own agendas.

People spend a lot of money 'learning' to talk – in presentation skills, influencing and negotiating, leadership, assertiveness and media training courses. Conversation analysis and skills training remain largely therapeutic and academic concerns. It is unrealistic to expect to talk fluently and persuasively in meetings and presentations and on the media if you neglect to interpret and refine your talk skills in everyday conversation. This chapter has two main themes:

- first, that much of our day-to-day conversation is built on messages and devices to do with status.

- second, that through understanding how talk works we can choose to play high or low status as appropriate. We can also identify what others are doing to play high status, and control our reactions.

To examine the tactics of talk we need first to consider . . .

WHAT TALK IS

Talk is shaped by language. Some linguistic scholars believe that language shapes thought, rather than vice versa. Certainly what we talk about and our ability to make ourselves understood is hampered or helped by the language we have at our disposal. And different languages have words that are exclusive to them and not readily translatable: the Greek word *hubris* for instance, meaning god-challenging, excessive pride (a sense of super-status – back to the Guinness defendants again), or the Welsh word *hiraeth*, meaning a poignant longing for the homeland. Cultural themes and values are expressed through the scope of words.

The way in which we use language reflects the preoccupations of society, of organisations and of individuals. For instance, in the business-orientated 1980s the phrase 'the bottom line' came into common usage. In the more uncertain 1990s, softer phrases like 'adding value' and 'creating synergy' became business buzzwords. Someone who frequently uses phrases like 'I think', 'in the final analysis' or 'the facts are' is indicating a different bent from the speaker who uses 'I feel', 'in increasing awareness' and 'let's imagine that'.

We talk to:

- Express ourselves and to make ourselves understood by others. We use words to give voice to our thoughts and feelings and to attempt to convey them to other people.

- Give and gain information. Some talkers do this as a large part of their jobs – teachers, policemen, doctors and management consultants, for instance. You may regard the 'talk' you do at work as mainly having this function; a lot of people do. This implies that people at work operate as robots, devoid of emotional involvement with one another. This viewpoint can be tempered by an appreciation of how we talk to . . .

- Create, destroy, change and reinforce relationships. Through talking we attempt to increase understanding, to express some of our needs and hopes, to influence, persuade and motivate others.

Most significantly for the theme of this book we talk to:

- Conceal our desires, hide our vulnerability or confusion. In other words we talk to maintain or elevate our apparent status. Much of our talk is veiled and indirect. To describe the underlying messages I've borrowed a term from script-writing, the sub-text, which describes the intentions and motivation behind the words. (Harold Pinter's scripts in particular are fine examples of dense orchestration of sub-text.)

WHAT'S YOUR SUB-TEXT?

Let's take talk at what many would consider its most mundane level: social chit-chat. Dave meets Andy for the first time and says

'Nice to meet you.' Depending on how Dave makes this greeting, it has a certain meaning. If Dave is looking over Andy's shoulder for someone more influential to talk to, then his sub-text is 'I'm being cursorily polite until I see someone better.' If Dave looks interested in Andy and smiles encouragingly, his sub-text reads, 'I'm looking forward to chatting with you.' Behaviour and voice signals behind the verbal camouflage convey much of the meaning.

So why do we lie to this extent? What prevents us addressing each other directly? When you meet someone for the first time, that person can

- Reject you.
- Overpower you.
- Accept you.

And you in turn can choose to do the same. Now you may be thinking that these options sound very dramatic and limited in the context of social chit-chat. You'd have a point. There are all sorts of options for how people can respond to one another when they first meet. The other person could flirt with you, for instance (if your luck was in), or flatter you or encourage you. For most of us, though, these responses are not nearly as threatening as the possibility of being rejected or overpowered.

As children, our cries for attention are acknowledged and responded to, ignored or dealt with by aggression. As adults, too, we remain familiar to these responses when we talk to others. We are strongly motivated by the need for love, which always carries with it the risk of rejection and withdrawal of that love. In giving and gaining love we seek closeness and involvement with other people. We are motivated, too, by the need to assert our individuality, to get our wants and desires fulfilled. This puts us on a delicately balanced see-saw. In seeking closeness our wants and desires, our need for self-expression, may be overpowered. In seeking love, the expression of our wants and desires may cause the other person to reject us.

The nature of social chit-chat, then, and indeed of the bulk of our talk, must be tentative and indirect. We need to pretend that the threats of being rejected and overpowered do not exist. We do not wish to appear vulnerable; we want to look good. We hedge about, sensing how close we can get to someone, and how much of ourselves we can risk revealing. We want to maintain our sense of status.

Besides these needs for involvement, and independence, we have others – like sex, for one. If we were to express this need openly and directly in social chit-chat we would risk offending others and we could expect a strong reaction in terms of them rejecting, over-powering or accepting us (in this instance their luck could be in). In Britain, where there is a high level of indirectness in social conversa-tion, subjects that smack of needs and beliefs – like sex, politics, religion and money – are often fastidiously avoided.

We adapt and suppress our needs in order to behave in a civilised fashion. In superficial conversation, on the surface at least we accept the image that the other person presents. It's impolite to challenge their integrity, the veracity of their self-expression. We cannot leap in and say, 'You seem nervous/alluring/self-obsessed.' We would provoke inappropriate responses. And, besides, we need love and approval – and the intrusive nature of these comments could well preclude that.

The more heavily disguised our needs, the less the risk of being rejected or overpowered – the more easily we can say, 'You misun-derstood me.' When the other person is an unknown commodity and we cannot predict how they will react, the greater is our requirement for the armour of indirectness.

SMALL TALK AND SUB-TEXT

'How do you do?', 'Nice to meet you', 'Hi, how are you?', 'Did you have a good journey?' 'All the best', 'Ciao', 'So long', 'See you, then', 'Do come again, soon', 'See you soon, I hope', 'Have a nice day'. In conversation, just like in air travel, arrivals and departures can be difficult, confusing interactions. To cover our confusion and to keep our emotional needs under control we deal with them by using stock phrases. These clichés effectively cover our embarrass-ment and maintain our status. Along with behaviour rites such as shaking hands, kissing, taking and giving of coats and getting drinks, they form rituals that make our meetings and partings easier.

Some readers may find 'small talk' difficult. As small talk is so indirect, you may have a sense that it's pretentious and dishonest. Perhaps you regard the main function of talk to be giving informa-tion directly and honestly. You may view yourself as a 'straight talker' – someone who uses words sparingly and appropriately to convey significant messages. If so, I'd like to suggest that you consider the main purpose of small talk. Through small talk, we demonstrate that we wish to get involved with other people (and, recluses aside, we all have this need); we establish relationships, we discover similarities and differences, and we build rapport and understanding. The beginning of conversation with strangers is all about finding something in common – or, to put it more succinctly, discovering commonality.

And the words we use are a small part of the process. You may discover early on in an interaction through words that you share common ground (that you both went to the same school, for instance). As important, though, will be more intangible commonality: a sense of humour, a cynical attitude, an acquisitive personality.

Effective small talk often runs to a formula. The overall direction of small talk is that it starts in the general and becomes more specific. Then the formula is:

- Make an innocuous statement.
- Follow it with a question that involves the other person.

An example:

> *Dave*: There are more people than I expected here. How come you're here?
> *Andy*: I'm the marketing manager for the company. And you?
> *Dave*: I'm one of your suppliers. Dave Smith. I supply most of your stationery.
> *Andy*: Then you'll have dealt with my office. Did we just get some new recycled stuff from you?
> *Dave*: That's right . . . (*and so on*).

POWER PLAY IN CONVERSATION

Warning: This next section could dramatically change your approach to conversation.

> 'If other people are going to talk, then conversation is simply impossible.'
>
> *James McNeill Whistler*

To build and maintain personal power, talking well helps. And understanding the values of self-expression and commonality are what talking well is about. This statement flies in the face of what many regard as powerful behaviour. The widespread belief is that to build status you need to bulldoze everyone else – your self-expression and agenda should dominate; you operate by overpowering others. But what happens then is that people stop telling you things. You make decisions in an isolated, ego-gratifying manner. Your information supplies become depleted. You cannot capitalise on other people's good ideas. You fail to take into consideration subordinates/customers/clients/your nearest and dearest. You stop getting support, and your influence is diminished. The need for excessive control in conversation can come from a deep fear that other people's ideas are threatening. To prevent them being expressed, you stage a pre-emptive strike.

Personal power involves receiving attention and recognition. To gain attention and recognition we need to be able to attend to and recognise others. Acquiring power is about learning to influence others and to feel in control of situations. Security in your power comes from learning to spot the control tactics of others, to resist them and to use them yourself where appropriate. To do this, you need to be able to understand how power games work in conversation, and what devices are used. The following guide to the tactics of talk is divided into two sections: Talk Tactics and Control, and Talk Tactics and Commonality. Some of the tactics used to control and involve are the same; but the sub-text – the intentions behind them – differs.

TALK TACTICS AND CONTROL

Here are twelve talk tactics that we use to gain control:

- *Dominating the conversation*
  By talking a lot, loudly, and expressing strong opinions early on, and frequently. If you're after domination, it's also immensely satisfying to have the last word in a conversation.
  Sub-text: I am an important person who deserves to be listened to. What I think is more important than the reactions of others.
  Comment: The bane of the quiet dinner *à deux* you were looking forward to in your local French restaurant, and of that meeting which you hoped would reach a rapid resolution.

- *Remaining uninvolved in the conversation*
  By contributing little, listening impassively without showing response or encouragement to the speaker to continue.
  Sub-text: 'I am evaluating you and disinclined to reveal my responses.' Or even 'I wish I wasn't here.'
  Comment: Behaviour used by people who feel uneasy with their status, and find that this 'low reaction' often intimidates others. Can be useful behaviour in negotiation. A favourite of some chief executives.

- *Frequent interrupting and talking over others*
  Useful overpowering tactic. Can be motivated by enthusiasm.
  Sub-text: 'I have to convey my message, which is more important than yours (and I may not be listening to you).'
  Comment: Research shows that men interrupt women far more than they do other men. Women interrupt men to a far lesser extent. In a typical doctor–patient exchange, a doctor will make on average six times as many interruptions as the patient. Any doubt still that status controls conversation?

- *Asking a lot of questions*
  Rapid-fire questions can seem like an interrogation. Questions can be very controlling: for instance, 'Why don't we go out?' means that the answer has to be well reasoned out. They can also really put people on the spot: 'Shouldn't you do that?' (really a command), 'Why has this happened?' (needing justification).
  Sub-text: 'I have the power to quiz you, and your discomfort at finding this intrusive does not matter.'
  Comment: Questions can be used for overt displays of snobbery, especially in culture, travel and fashion. 'Have you read the latest Antonia Byatt?/been to Rajastan?' Or, as someone recently asked me, 'Do you think Jasper Conran is the new Yves St Laurent?' Questions like this may be asked by people who assume that you have the same sort of lifestyle as they do, or who are clumsily trying to find out whether you do.

- *Giving advice*
  'Speak up', 'Don't worry', 'In your place I'd . . .', 'You could try . . .'. There is something enormously satisfying in giving another person advice, especially if they appear to take it seriously. Relentless advice-giving can diminish the other person's status, in

that it implies they need it. When advice becomes orders, the other person's will is overpowered.

Sub-text: 'Mother knows best.'

Comment: Lots of us do this for a living.

- *Interpreting and judging*
  'Men are aggressive', 'He's not giving you enough space', 'The problem is money', 'I know exactly how you feel', 'It'll never happen.' Impossible not to do. There, I've just done it. We like to make sense of things, to analyse, to generalise, to see ourselves as rational problem solvers.

  Sub-text: I am a skilled interpreter who makes sense of things – better than you do. You mean what I would mean if I used those words.

  Comment: Some of us would like to be psychoanalysts.

- *Criticising and praising*
  'What a lovely little room', 'I'm not that keen on the food here', 'You *have* done well', 'I prefer your hair that way.' Criticism connected to choices we have made – about restaurants, films, books to read – may be interpreted as reflecting on the person who made the choice or suggestion, though this may not be the critic's intention. Another subtle form of criticism occurs when someone else is lavishly praised and you're left to make a comparison: 'That report Angela's done is truly excellent' (sub-text: 'It's a shame yours wasn't').

  Sub-text: 'My relative status compared to yours entitles me to criticise or praise you.'

  Comment: Used widely throughout our lives to assert status – by parents, children, spouses, teachers, trainers and those we work with/for.

- *Giving sympathy*
  'Oh you poor thing, how awful for you', 'Don't go through that experience again alone – give us a call – we're here to help.' If you're dealing with someone who plays 'victim' to get by in life, then this will be just what they're after. And they might use the sympathy (and sense of guilt that you're better off than they are) you feel towards them to control *you*. People frequently give sympathy where it's not wanted – where the other person perhaps regards themselves as strong, determined, a fighter.

Liberal doses of sympathy compromise the other person's self-image.

Sub-text: 'I'm in a stronger position in that I can feel sorry for you, and you are vulnerable. If I can keep you down, I stay up.'

Comment: We often react in this way when we're unsure what emotional needs the other person is expressing, and how to deal with them.

- *Anecdotes that bolster self-image*

  'And I said to him, "Push off, mate, I'm not standing for that" – and he did, pretty quickly!', 'I cleared out my wardrobe at the weekend – and took a stack of clothes down to Oxfam.' Some of us constantly tell stories where we depict ourselves as having the qualities we secretly think we lack or that others need reminding of.

  Sub-text: 'I am admirable.'

  Another version of this tactic is to refer everything back to yourself, to personalise every topic. And if the topic is something that you can't personalise, then you change the direction of the conversation so that you can: 'Back to what you were saying earlier, when that happened to me, I . . .'. If that fails, you may decide to disengage from the conversation.

  Sub-text: 'My experience is extremely significant.'

  Comment: Self-deprecating stories are often funny, and get us liked by others as they indicate we don't take ourselves too seriously.

- *Name dropping, recalling credentials, using jargon, excluding others*

  'I said to Salman the other day' (uttered at a dinner party I attended), 'When I was director of marketing. . . .', 'I'm obsessing when I want to be impacting.' Blatant attempts at suggesting status and covering up inadequacies are used all the time in the business world – to show connections and influence, establish a good track record or to create a mystique about something. If you want to get the boss's ear it may mean excluding other people from the conversation, although they are still present.

  Sub-text: 'I need to impress.'

  Comment: Watch out for salesmen who use jargon to imply superior knowledge and understanding. Having created confusion, they can then give advice in order to control the sale.

- *Sending cryptic messages*
  'There will be changes in company structure in the autumn', 'Yes, Jane mentioned you were feeling a little under par at the meeting', 'Watch your back with him' and, as told to an actor post-performance in the dressing room by a friend and rival, 'What about you, then?' Cryptic speech makes the most of the indirect nature of talk. Messages are very heavily veiled so that interpretation is difficult. When cryptic messages are used threateningly they play on fears – of being inadequate, of not having job security, of having limited knowledge and understanding. Unwittingly, sometimes, cryptic speech is used by people who have great trouble being direct. Talking cryptically carries the insurance policy of being able to say, 'You misinterpreted me.'
  Sub-text: 'I have the power to predict, to warn you, to threaten you, to criticise you, but I choose to give you this message in a very subtle way. It's up to you whether you think you're using sharp powers of interpretation or acting according to paranoia. I am unable to expand upon this message.'
  Comment: Pernicious. Know what I mean?

- *Dodging and diminishing*
  'Oh, you'll be fine', 'You've still got that problem with Max? . . . This room needs a coat of paint, don't you think?', 'I'll tell you a funny story about that'. We can maintain control of conversation by avoiding other people's agendas. For instance, if you've got a problem that you're keen to talk about and I rush in to reassure you that it's not a problem, I dodge your agenda. I might offer a clichéd solution: 'No use crying over spilt milk.' If I suddenly transfer my attention to an object or some aspect of the physical environment (after all, inanimate things are much easier to deal with, aren't they – they don't have emotions) when you're revealing thoughts and feelings, then once again I've dodged your agenda. And if I use humour to avoid your problem or make light of it, then I diminish its significance. I command you not to take yourself so seriously. Sarcasm and ridicule are humorous forms of criticism – the perpetrator has the get-out clause: 'I was only joking.'
  Sub-text: 'I'm choosing the direction of this conversation.'
  Comment: We avoid embarrassment, and involvement in other people's problems by dodging and diminishing. We maintain our status by concealing our inability to help others.

DEALING WITH CONTROL TACTICS:
COUNTER-STRATEGY

Transcripts of conversation reveal that involved parties switch from one control tactic to another, and that different tactics effectively counter one another. For example:

Jennifer: I think we should go with the offer. It's the best we're going to get, and if we don't take it now we won't have another. [*Judging.*]

Helen: Shouldn't we wait a couple of months? [*Giving advice through a question.*]

Jennifer: No. I know this is tough on you – I'm sorry for the pressure you're going to be under, you poor old thing. [*Sympathising.*]

Helen: Oh, don't worry about little old me – I'll be all right. [*Dodging.*] Why do you want to act now? [*Questioning.*]

When both parties are actively seeking control and using similar tactics, the conversation can escalate into conflict or a competition. If Jennifer continued to ladle the sympathy on Helen, the latter might tactically have brought into the conversation something that she knows to be a vulnerable area for Jennifer. Helen would then seize the opportunity to use the controlling tactic of sympathy on Jennifer. For instance:

Jennifer: I think the time is right. I've trusted my instincts in the past and they've usually been right. I'll give you lots of support –

Helen: Is this a good time for you to do this, though? So soon after the company restructure?

Jennifer: Yes, I think so, I –

Helen: You don't want to get ill again. We felt so sorry for you at the shareholders' meeting. [*Sympathy from Helen, with the sub-text: 'Got you!'*]

Here are some suggestions for countering control tactics:

- *The dominator*
  Comment on what's going on. Use talk analysis. When strong opinions are being expressed, ask for reasons. 'Can I have my say, please?', 'Can I ask you why you hold that opinion so vociferously?', 'I need to say something.' Interrupt – difficult to do if you've been brought up to be polite, but necessary to learn.

Dodging through wry humour works, too: 'I don't think the next
door office have quite your entire thesis on this subject.'

- *The evaluator*
  Ask for their opinion: 'What do you think of what I've said so
  far?' And if that is responded to cryptically ('OK'), then ask for
  advice. Most of us, especially when seeking control, can't resist
  giving advice.

- *The interruptor*
  Analyse again. 'May I say my piece and then hear yours?', 'Can
  we both stop talking at once?' Interrupt back, but more loudly,
  and include praise: 'That's an excellent point you're making
  there and I'd like to say that . . .'. This counter-tactic works very
  well with most people. You acknowledge their status and they'll
  be quite happy to bask in reflected glory for a while as you say
  your piece. You may even convert them to an ally.

- *The interrogator*
  Ask open questions back – that is, ones that require longer
  answers like questions beginning with 'How?' (which can seem
  challenging). 'How d'you come to be here today?' If questions
  are used to assert superiority ('Have you been to Rajastan?') then
  you can disarm the questioner by using real or feigned naivety.
  'No, where is it?'

- *The adviser*
  State what you want. 'I'm not asking for advice, but I want to
  talk through something with you. Can I do that?', 'I'd be happier
  making up my own mind about this – thanks for your interest.'
  And again analyse: 'You're giving me a lot of advice here from
  your viewpoint – I need to plot my own course.'

- *The judge*
  Ask for motives: 'On what basis are you making that interpretation?', 'What are your reasons for holding that view?' Use
  humour: 'Gosh, you've got me analysed', 'I didn't know you'd
  studied psychology', 'My, but you are decisive.' Let the other
  person know that you know they're not God. 'So this is your
  opinion?'

- *The critic*
  Ask for specific description: 'What specifically was wrong with
  the report?' Ask for motivation: 'How come you're mentioning

the report now?' And the cruncher for dealing with excessive criticism or praise: 'Thank you for saying that.' If someone is hell-bent on controlling you through criticism you stop them by agreeing with what they say ('Yes, you're quite right about the report') and then remaining quiet. Be sure, though, that you don't use this just because a need to control and not to appear vulnerable prevents you accepting criticism in any form.

- *The sympathiser*
'You can disarm people who use sympathy as a control tactic by emphasising the positive and again analysing your position. 'Thank you for your sympathy, but that's not really what I'm after. The situation has its plus side, you know. I'm meeting lots of new people, and since the divorce I've thrown myself into my job.'

- *The cryptic commentator*
Ask gently, without appearing defensive, for further information. Be persistent. Better to lose face and be open about not understanding the cryptic message, than to lose sleep at night over it. If further information is not available, establish a time when it will be. Use the same tactic to deal with name dropping and use of jargon: 'I don't understand who/what you're talking about.' If you're being excluded from the conversation, concentrate on listening supportively and in an interested manner.

- *The braggart*
Anecdotes that bolster self-image reveal a great deal to you about the speaker. Use that information. Remember the anecdote about the actor who, after talking about himself at length, then says, 'But that's enough about me, let's talk about you – what do you think of me?' Flattery also works here – if you want to say something about yourself, suggest to the speaker that you're choosing them to confide in.

- *The artful dodger*
Again, analysis of the situation can help: 'We've got away from what I wanted to discuss – can we go back to it?' Using 'we' as opposed to 'I' suggests collective responsibility for dodging and diminishing. If the dodging is being done to ignore expressed emotion, then keep expressing it: 'Can I say again how anxious I feel about this?'

TALK TACTICS AND COMMONALITY

To talk well, we need to take and surrender control during conversation. And finding commonality involves conquering any fear that the other person poses a threat, and allowing them 'airtime'. If you are someone who constantly uses control tactics, the following list will be helpful to you.

In the next section I aim to show that the tactics of finding commonality are used as much to assert status as are the tactics of control. You may pride yourself on being a generous listener who is very interested in others, and use this pride to excuse you from using control tactics. Perhaps the threat of being rejected or overpowered by others, and experiences in your conditioning, lead you to avoid controlling. If you don't go up in your plane, there's no risk of being shot down. To encourage commonality we:

- *Disclose a great deal*
  'Gosh, I'm so sorry I'm late, I've had a terrible journey and on top of that I've got the flu. I'm really very sorry – I'm completely disorganised this morning.' Disclosing things about yourself often encourages other people to open up too. But in inappropriate situations and when talking with someone who is quite guarded, over-disclosure may be interpreted as intrusive. Do you really answer the question, 'How are you?'
  Sub-text: 'I'm emotionally overloaded, so I'm going to dump some on you. I'm revealing so much about myself as I'm an example you should follow. I'm really well adjusted so I can let it all hang out. Why can't you?'
  Comment: This can be a protective tactic and can embarrass and undermine the other person.

- *Talking too much*
  When nervous, some of us talk too much. We sense that during pauses assessments are being made, and we don't like this. Some of us see proof of good relationships in endless chatter without breaks. Others see proof of the same in little need to talk, sitting in empathetic silence together.

- *Apologising for ourselves*
  Apologising and being self-deprecating can let you off the hook. You're not into playing apparent high status. People can think as badly of you as you do of yourself.

Sub-text: 'Have no expectations of me, and then I won't let you down. I am low-status so you can't do anything to diminish me. I'm instructing you how to respond to me.'

Comment: Very useful device when you want to ingratiate yourself with another person who is trying hard to play high status. But they could, of course, take it to indicate that they can trample all over you.

- *Reflective listening*
  A counselling technique, where the listener does not pass judgement or give advice, but focuses all attention on the speaker. The listener indicates that they're listening through non-verbal signals, mms and aahs, stretched out final syllables ('and th-e-n'), paraphrasing and summarising. Thoughts and feelings behind the words are interpreted. It's a deceptively simple idea that's very difficult to put into practice.
  Sub-text: 'I am here for you, to act as a sounding board expressing empathy. My agenda does not matter (though I maintain my status in not revealing anything about myself). I'm acting as your analyst (and isn't this extremely generous of me as you're not paying?).
  Comment: Isn't life too short to listen to some people?

- *Being over-polite*
  A lot of us are brought up not to talk too much about ourselves, not to interrupt, not to talk about certain subjects. At all costs we must avoid appearing to want attention and to cause controversy. Some of us are reserved good listeners who see our prime function in conversation as encouraging the other person. We wish to be seen as sensitive and considerate towards others. 'Please, what were you going to say next?' 'No, after you.'
  Sub-text: 'I'm not making myself vulnerable, I don't want to deal with the unpredictable or get close to you.'
  Comment: Politeness can create distance. If you're over-polite in conversation, your use of distance may suggest that you want to play high status by keeping the other person at bay, below you. When the other person is less formal and more forthcoming, he or she may well feel compromised by their self-disclosure which has not been reciprocated. They may have a sense of reduced status. Stiff, formal politeness sometimes helps us cope with situations in which we feel awkward. If you choose to abandon formality ('Why don't we discuss this over a drink?') then you are

playing high status in that you're taking this decision, and allowing the other person perhaps to rise above their station.

- *Advising, passing judgement, criticising, praising, flattering*
Most frequently we do this to people we are close to, and to people with whom we think we've got a lot in common. After all, we want to help them. And it does take courage to do these things, as well as a belief that you are, of course, right.
Sub-text: 'I'm only doing this for your own good, to be helpful. You're just like me, I understand you.'
Comment: You may be offering closeness and commonality that's not reciprocated and is overpowering. Telling stories that describe how you had a similar experience fall into the same camp. When you flatter people, you acknowledge their status. Praise can often disguise the sub-text 'I want to be more like you, and I am envious of what you have.' When the praise is lavish, the receiver may interpret the speaker's sub-text to be: 'You have low self-esteem and magnanimous me will build it up.' The intention is to patronise.

- *Use indirect questions*
'Can I do anything to help?', 'Are you doing anything tonight?', 'What do you think of my hair?', 'How are you?' We ask indirect questions so that we do not cause offence or impose on other people. These questions are often opening gambits for a negotiation of some sort, even if it's just for interest and approval from one another. We have expectations or scenarios in our heads about how they will be answered. So for instance:

> *Anne*: Are you doing anything tonight?
> *Mark*: Yes, I'm playing football.
> *Anne*: Oh [*feels miffed, status diminished, he's not considering her like she's considering him*].
>   *Her imagined scenario was*:
> *Anne*: Are you doing anything tonight?
> *Mark*: No, what would you like to do?
> *Anne*: Go to the Italian restaurant [*her status and need for control acknowledged, without her needing to sound bossy or assertive*].

Sub-text: 'I matter so much and my feelings are so important that you are able to read my mind.'
Comment: Indirect questions are used all the time by people

who need their status boosting through being given buckets of approval, or who are looking for a reason for punishing other people should they not fall in with the anticipated scenario.

- *Showing involvement through strong responses*
  'Wow, really exciting!', 'God, how utterly appalling!', 'You're really terrific!' Conveying enthusiasm and reaction is done to show involvement. But if the other party doesn't use this level of response themselves, they may regard you as insincere or phoney. They may feel patronised.
  Sub-text: 'I need to be expressive here so that the person will like me. This person is not very sensitive, so they need to register strong reactions.'
  Comment: Can also make the other person think that you lack powers of discrimination.

- *Complaining*
  'Isn't it hot here?' 'The boss is really getting to all of us, now.' Voicing of complaints can be done by someone who assumes the status of acting as collective mouthpiece.
  Sub-text: 'Everyone else is feeling the same as me.'
  Comment: Sometimes mistakenly done to create commonality by people who assume that others share their grievances. Moaners get attention but they're not much fun to have around!

- *Humour*
  'Have you heard the one about . . .?' Humour is known as 'the great leveller'. It is, provided that other people share your sense of humour and the timing is appropriate.
  Sub-text: 'Let's not get heavy here . . . life's a funny business.' 'You shouldn't take it so seriously . . .'
  Comment: When you make other people laugh, you defend yourself against them taking you too seriously. You're less likely to be criticised for what you really believe in.

- *Sending cryptic messages*
  This has to be the best of the commonality tactics. It plays heavily on indirectness, intimacy and common understanding.
  Sub-text: 'We both know what we're talking about here.'
  An example:
  > *Sally*: I'd better go soon.
  > *William*: Do you have to? Have you got an early start?

Sally: No, not especially. It's just, well . . . maybe I'll stay a little longer.

William: Yes, have another drink. I usually get an alarm call. . . .

No comment.

DEALING WITH COMMONALITY TACTICS:
COUNTER-STRATEGY

Commonality tactics are frequently used unconsciously to lower the other person's status. This occurs when the speaker fails to appreciate the differences between speaker and listener. The speaker assumes that the listener shares the speaker's need for closeness and the view that both parties have a lot in common.

These tactics are also used a great deal to achieve the user's disguised objective. The salesperson who shows great interest in you, for instance, and probes gently to find out about you: who listens receptively, with a lot of head nodding, so that you start nodding too, and continue to nod when the sales contract and pen are put in your hand.

Here is some counter-strategy to deal with commonality tactics. If someone is:

- *Talking too much, over-disclosing*
  Ask closed questions which require yes, no or one-word answers. Shift the conversation to a less personal topic.

- *Apologising*
  Ask them why they are apologising, or inform them that they don't need to: 'Why are you apologising?', 'Please don't apologise for yourself.'

- *Listening reflectively*
  When someone is doing this it is very difficult to gain commitment. Ask them specifically for their advice or opinion.

- *Being over-polite*
  Analyse what's going on. Disclose that you are finding the proceedings formal and ask if the other person minds being more informal. A change of environment, from board-room to bar, say, may help.

- *Praising, showing strong responses*
  When you suspect that someone is flattering you in order to manipulate, or responding in an artificial manner, ask for specific detail. 'What was it about the report that you found so interesting, for future reference?' If the praise is genuine, the giver should be able to be specific. In this instance you may be regarded as falling short in the modesty stakes, as your question may be interpreted to mean that you want even more adulation. Your decision to use this ploy depends on whether or not you think such a misinterpretation is preferable to being conned.

- *Using indirect questions*
  Try to get the other person to be as specific as possible. 'Are you doing anything tonight?' could be followed by 'Yes, but it's not a definite commitment. What would you like to do?' Be forthcoming, and hope that this tactic becomes contagious.

- *Complaining*
  When another person is complaining as a collective voice and you don't agree with their grievance, then voice your opinion. Your silence may be taken to mean tacit agreement.

By now you should have an idea of the talk tactics that you and others use to play power games. If you are someone who is interpreted as aggressive and would like to be less so, you can increase your adaptability for different situations and people by using commonality tactics. But if you come across as a push-over, albeit a likeable one (but not someone who commands respect), study and use the control tactics. Specific points to concentrate on in either situation are described below.

Using Talk Tactics

Our responses to talk tactics are dictated by how we believe we should react to others. Some of us are far more comfortable asserting our power through control, while others will be more comfortable seeking commonality. Which of the above tactics do you make most use of?

Under pressure, we tend to use that which is familiar and comfortable. Some people assert their power almost exclusively through control tactics, and find it almost impossible to ask questions that are not disguised advice or judgement. They cannot ask another person an open question along the lines of 'What do you think/feel about this?' Unconsciously, they may regard those sort of questions as intrusive or threatening, in that the other person may not say what they wish to hear.

Learning to Use Commonality Tactics

If you are one of those who habitually use control tactics, you may wish to increase your adaptability with others and extend your range of influence through using commonality tactics. And the more people you influence, the higher your status. When you're not getting anywhere with someone, you can choose to switch streams. Focus specifically on:

- *Using open questions*
  Listen to answers and respond to what's been said, rather than force your own agenda. Clarify and summarise what's been said and pick up on points in stories: 'And then?'

- *Active listening*
  Give others your attention and concentrate on what they're saying. Let your body language, eye contact and facial expression show involvement and receptivity. Remind yourself that you can evaluate what's been said, and take time to consider it. You don't have to leap in and pass judgement or give advice immediately.

- *Disclosing information*
  Give others nuggets of information about yourself and take them into your confidence. This doesn't mean exposing yourself so that you become vulnerable. But if you reveal some of your experience and history, others will trust you more readily and be more willing to open up themselves.

Learning to Use Control Tactics

If, on the other hand, you are someone who restricts themselves to using commonality tactics, you may end up as a martyr. This is self-defeating unless you believe that being constantly quashed by the talk tactics of others means that you'll go to heaven. Take the lead in conversation through:

- *Expressing your opinions and feelings*
  If others disagree, they are not necessarily attacking you as a person, only your viewpoint. And some people misguidedly use disagreement with others as the main instrument of asserting their status.

- *Curbing responses that may be interpreted as compliant and acquiescing*
  For instance, if you are listening to someone and you are not sure whether you agree with their content, measure your behaviour. Instead of nodding enthusiastically, saying 'yes', 'aaha' and smiling a great deal, continue to listen attentively but use words like 'perhaps', 'maybe' and 'that's possible' to show that you are also assessing the content.

- *Stand up for yourself*
  Appreciating and considering others does not mean that you neglect to do these things for yourself. Use analysis of the situation you are in as your key tactic: 'I've not been able to make my point. Can I, please?', 'I want to say something without interruption. Can I do that, please?', 'I have views which I would like to express.'

THE LANGUAGE OF POWER

'Is that Mr Davies? Good morning, Mr Davies. This is Dr Rees speaking.' Through our use of titles we keep people at a distance. Dropping off titles and surnames indicates greater familiarity. And allowing someone to call you by your first name ('Please, call me John') has the sub-text: 'I am higher-status than you are and so can grant you this permission.'

Some of us play God through our use of language. We assert 'the facts are', 'the case is' and 'the truth is' when what we really mean is 'I interpret the facts to mean', 'my opinion is' or 'I think.' 'God-speak' often sounds pompous and bombastic and the sub-text can suggest: 'I'm not really confident about my thoughts and opinions, so I'll couch them as holy proclamations.' In a sense, then, this use of language is low-status play, though you may acquire some disciples who are sufficiently intimidated by your 'divine intervention'.

Through implication, language can diminish or elevate the status of others. Many women resent being addressed as 'my dear', feeling patronised by the sense of ownership and familiarity conveyed through the description. Avuncular men in their fifties and sixties may not be aware that this term of endearment causes such a reaction; you could enlighten them by telling them that the form of address is out-of-date and out-of-favour these days. A more extreme tactic is to start addressing them in similar vein – using 'my dear' or something worse back (at a seminar I attended, 'baby' was suggested . . . but if it's your boss you're dealing with you may need to decide whether your job's worth it). Addressing someone as 'young man' or 'old boy', shortening their name without their consent, or calling them by their surname alone, are all instances where forms of address may be used to denote the speaker's higher status.

Language is also used to create mystique. When computer salespeople start talking about bytes and mice, beware. They are playing on the fact that most of us do not like to appear ignorant or ill informed. They are talking a language we probably do not understand, and which they hope will impress us and befuddle us and increase their power. The next tactic they use is to give us advice. They enlighten us on the mystery, we are grateful to them, we trust them and then we buy their product.

While all this is going on, the computer salesperson will repeatedly use the customer's Christian name: 'Now, John, you see that when I do this with the mouse. . . . John, why don't you have a go?' They do this to make us feel that we are significant – they are recognising the customer as an individual. The customer is made to feel that her or his status is acknowledged.

Gentle reader, here are some counter-tactics. Jargon is an effective form of shorthand, provided everyone understands it. If you don't understand what someone is describing, ask what they mean. It doesn't have to sound confrontational; contrast 'I don't understand what you're talking about' (sub-text: 'you are inept at talking') with 'I'm sorry I'm so dim [mock disclosure – and quite appropriate in my opinion, given the indirect nature of conversation], but could you explain that to me again in plain English?' (sub-text: 'I'm not understanding you, so can you say it differently?')

When, gentle reader, someone over-uses your name as a controlling tactic, a throwaway comment disguising an analysis of what is going on can be most effective: 'Gosh, it's interesting how you call me by my Christian name so much' (sub-text: 'I've rumbled you – stop it'). Or you can play the same game back: 'Now, Mr X, can you tell me the price, please . . . and then, Mr X, the payment terms?'

Now, gentle reader, I expect at my third reference to you as 'gentle reader' you're starting to feel rather less than gentle towards me. Aren't I playing high status in that I can tell you who you are? We use adjectives to belittle or increase people's status and to create associations between their status as individuals and their attributes and possessions. 'You're such a sweet little thing', 'You're a big boy' (more often thought than said aloud), 'I got your little report' (sub-text: 'from little you') 'What a magnificent office' (sub-text: 'and aren't you a magnificent person sitting in it?').

When Neil Kinnock led the Labour party, he was advised to stop using 'Hello, love' and 'Hi, kid' as forms of address in public. He was especially fond of using the latter when addressing old age pensioners. This use of language reflected his accessible, informal, spontaneous campaigning style. It's difficult to imagine his rival, Margaret Thatcher, saying 'Hi, kid' to anyone. In their two contrasting styles we return to the main theme of this chapter: the Kinnock style emphasising commonality and the Thatcher theme emphasising control.

SHYNESS AND POWER

In a social context, it can be difficult to assert personal power and gain recognition if you're shy. Your shyness may, of course, help you achieve status in other areas. If you're striving to write a great novel or to invent a piece of computer software, the very shyness that makes you avoid social events may allow you more time and motivation to pursue your solitary goals. For most of us, though, gaining recognition from others is to some extent dependent on our confidence in letting others know who we are and what we're about. So shyness can be a considerable impediment to power. And shyness is something that's linked to self-assurance, already mentioned in Chapter Two. Here's a piece of self-disclosure.

Several years ago I met someone who is now a very famous television celebrity and did a piece on the radio with them. The item went well, and it was reported to me that the celebrity was very pleased with my contribution. About two-and-a-half years later I walked into a small clothes shop to see the celebrity holding court. My instant response was that he would not remember who I was (poor old little insignificant me). Embarrassed at my ineptitude in the situation, I feigned great interest in a rack of clothes at the back of the shop. I became aware that the celebrity was looking at me fixedly (either trying to remember who I was, in expectation of acknowledgement, or in surprise that I should cut him dead in such a manner). I fumbled with the clothes, cringing. It was much too late for me to acknowledge him. I sidled out of the shop, mortified.

I had done what a lot of people do when struck with shyness – tried to detach myself from a situation because I anticipated rejection. Many shy people find the role of the detached evaluator a useful one: it gives them a sense of power over those people who need a lot of obvious approval, yet the role doesn't demand too much of a contribution from them. They can play at being still waters that run deep. The limitations of this role are considerable, and such people can hardly expect others to be receptive, forthcoming and responsive towards them.

There were several repercussions following my slight incident in the clothes shop. Since then, through third parties, two opportunities have come my way to work with that celebrity. Neither came to fruition, and I shall never know why. Suffice to say, the 'clothes shop débâcle' has assumed an inflated significance in my mind. It was a salutary lesson for me on risking rejection and on my perceived notions of status. With hindsight, I should have said 'Hallo' and then, if necessary, reminded him where we'd previously met.

Another useful role for the shy person is that of the 'good listener'. Undoubtedly, listening well is a vital conversational skill. But if you only listen well and make little contribution yourself, you risk suppressing your own needs and leaving the other party feeling cheated and exposed at the end of the conversation. After all, they were generous and kept throwing the ball at you – they played the game, but you didn't play back.

Here are some suggestions for dealing with shyness:

- 'Shy people are selfish' goes the saying, implying that such people

78

are too preoccupied with themselves. 'Shy people have an over-generous view of others' might be more accurate. When struck by shyness, we think that other people are very interested in us and evaluating us. In some situations, like interviews, this may be partially true. But lots of other agendas are being ignored, like the 'What's in it for me?' factor. In social situations, most of us want to enjoy ourselves through pleasant company and good food and wine. We may want to make useful contacts with others. Few of us (unless we are looking for this) want to become fixated with interest on another individual. So, remember, you're not *that* interesting. . . .

- Very little of what's said in conversation is direct and meaning-ful. There's an apocryphal story about former US President Franklin D. Roosevelt, that his opening gambit in chit-chat was often 'My grandmother's just died.' This was frequently received by comments like 'How nice' or 'Oh, really'. For the tongue-tied it's worth preparing some stock comments and even preparing for social chit-chat by noting interesting stories in the media. When you first trot these out, you may find that to your ears they sound artificial and contrived. Persevere, and they should become more natural. Remember the formula for social talk: an innocuous statement followed by a question moving from the general to the specific.

- Ask yourself 'What are the pay-offs of being shy, and do I have a vested interest in maintaining them?' As a shy child, you may have experienced shame and humiliation from people and situa-tions. In turn this may have led to you getting attention, protec-tion and sensitivity from some people. You may be still getting this cotton wool treatment, and may not want to relinquish it. If you choose to do so, then prepare for what may seem like tough responses.

- In his book *Coping with Blushing* Dr Robert Edelmann suggests replacing negative thoughts by positive ones, which takes time and considerable application. Repeat phrases such as 'I can cope', 'I can think rationally' and 'I can manage this situation.' Remind yourself that blushing is not the worst thing that can happen to you.

- Focusing on other people helps too. If you can choose whom to talk to, pick someone who looks as though they have something in common with you – be it gender, age or an aura of self-effacement similar to the one you are experiencing. Introduce yourself straightaway, smile, make direct eye contact and ask open questions which indicate your interest in the other person.

• Get yourself as relaxed as possible before going into daunting situations. Use breathing and relaxation exercises (see pp 164 and 171) to reduce physical tension.

• Disclosing what's happening to you can make you feel better and, as described earlier in this chapter, it can also raise your status: 'I feel quite tongue-tied in this company' or 'That comment's made me go quite red!' If this disclosure is made light-heartedly, so much the better. In doing this, you maintain status by showing that you are aware and not ashamed of what is going on. And many people will value your sensitivity.

GETTING IN AND OUT OF CONVERSATION

Tactfully joining in and getting out of conversation can be difficult. In the indirect business of conversation, it is as well to do it as skilfully as possible and without leaving others feeling awkward. Commenting on the process of communication can again help: 'Can I join your conversation?', 'Do you mind if I talk to you?', 'I've enjoyed talking to you. Please excuse me – I'm off for a refill', 'I'm enjoying our chat, but I've just seen someone whom I need to speak to urgently.' Avoid behaviour indicating sub-text like: 'You're boring me rigid and I'm looking for someone more interesting to talk to.' Other people don't need to be diminished by you in that way – and in any case it shows you're insecure about your own power.

chapter four

PERSONAL POWER
AT WORK

'What do you do?' asks the polite guest. You reply. When you tell her you're an estate agent, she tries to cover her contempt. When you tell her you're a doctor, she looks impressed. When you tell her you're a housewife/house-husband, she patronises you. She defines your status by what you do. In our society, with the erosion of class barriers as we used to know them job description is an important measure of social standing.

So one of the first things many of us seek to find out about other people is what they do. And occupational psychologists have shown that the definition of your job by others can affect your performance. If you can find meaning and reason for what you do and a sense of useful function, then your job will seem significant. The value that your job is given by other people can make it seem worthwhile. It gives you status.

Why do we work? Research into people's needs and motivation indicates that it's not just for the money – the financial aspect can be over-stressed. Paul McCartney and Madonna, Lord Hanson and Rupert Murdoch all have more money than they will ever need. Yet they continue to work. Why? For status and self-fulfilment needs, perhaps? In less lofty circles, pay rises do not compensate for changes in other conditions at work. This insight came from a cab-driver:

I've been on this circuit for six months now, but I've been driving cabs for twenty-four years. I had to leave my other company. They brought in this computerised call system which meant I took all my calls from a computer [*thumps dashboard*] here. Well, it really speeded things up and I was making quite a bit more, but I missed the chat. I mean, the caller and I – well, we've got a relationship. And it doesn't matter where I am, I can call him up. It's social, innit? Work's got to be social.

Money, though, is the most tangible indicator we have of the value of our work, and it is inextricably linked with status. When employees ask for more money it is a comparative exercise. If the management in a company get a pay rise, then it can be argued that the shop-floor workers should get one too. If nurses' jobs are given a certain value, then ambulance workers' and hospital porters' wages may be calculated by comparing their contribution with that of the nurses. The money we are paid is recognition for our status compared to that of other people.

Several studies have been made of people's needs and how they are satisfied by work (see Further Reading). Individuals have different needs, and these will differ according to their situation and time of life: a young graduate may have a strong need to sense that she or he fits into an organisation, while a middle-aged employee facing redundancy may have future security as a main priority. Our needs include:

- *Survival*
  To ensure our physical survival we need sex, food and drink. We need physical and psychological security, and we need money to buy these things. The psychologist Abraham Maslow concluded that, if these basic physical and security needs are not satisfied, it is difficult for us to fulfil our higher needs. We are motivated by our needs when they are not satisfied.

- *Relationships with others*
  To love and to be loved, to have friendship, to feel a sense of involvement and identification, to get recognition from others, to experience dependency and independence, to feel that we 'belong'.

- *Self-fulfilment*
  To respect and love ourselves, to be confident and powerful, to achieve our goals, to develop ourselves so that we realise our potential, to gain insight, to use our creativity.

Like the cab driver, it can be useful to assess your particular balance of needs and consider the extent to which they are being satisfied. This can be an especially useful consideration if you are unhappy in a job or about to change direction. Quite clearly, if you have a strong need for the company of others then a technical research job where you are largely left to your own devices may prove stressful – unless you do a lot of extra-curricular socialising as compensation. You would be better off in the personnel department. But if you are a strongly goal-orientated individual who enjoys solitary intellectual pursuits, you may have found the perfect job. These days employers are increasingly using psychometric testing (personality tests) to try and help them fit the personality to the job (see pp 96–97).

Note: Strong needs for relationships with others can be exploited. It's sometimes thought quite reasonable that women and the 'do-gooding' professions are poorly paid, as the social satisfaction of their work is so rewarding. The same thing applies to 'exclusive' jobs: 'You're so lucky to be: working in this posh Knightsbridge shop/meeting celebrity authors/the international jet-setter's PA – that you can be paid very little money for doing so.' The kudos of the job, the implied associations and the admiration of others are felt to be more than enough compensation.

JOB TITLES AND POWER

Over the years I've noticed 'job-title consciousness' increasing dramatically. When I meet a prospective new employee they often seem more concerned with their job title than they do with their salary. I've even had some negotiate over their job title, and once they've got that, conditions and pay don't seem to matter. Are we really so self-important?

Managing director of an electronics company

Power at work can be divided into two aspects, as already briefly explained in Chapter Eight:

- *Overt power*
  Conferred status and rank through job title, company car, number of subordinates, size of office and number of phones.

- *Active power*
  Far less tangible, but can be based on expert knowledge, social

skills, ability to influence, contacts, personal power, and knowledge of the organisation and its politics.

When someone first joins an organisation, it's much easier for them to ascertain their new colleagues' overt power than it is to understand their active power. And if you join an organisation where rank is clearly delineated and tightly structured, like the army, you can quickly get a sense of your place in things. But in business these days, with a loosening up of rigid authoritarian organisation and a 'flattening out' of structure, it's much more difficult. Perhaps some people's preoccupation with job titles on business cards is compensation for this.

Overt power can be a sham. While Ronald Reagan was President of the United States, real power lay with advisers like Caspar Weinberger, who wielded enormous behind-the-scenes influence. During the Thatcher years in Britain, few people were aware of Sir Alan Walter's significance in shaping economic policy until he fell out with the Chancellor, Nigel Lawson, who subsequently resigned. In business, an employee near retirement age may well be given a job with a grand title in a department which has little influence in the overall scheme of things. To be effective, overt power has to be backed up by active status.

Let's take a managerial position as an example. A manager is given a title in the formal organisation of the company. Within the company, even within his or her department, there will be informal groups and informal vying for power. If the manager runs a sales team where everyone has the job title 'sales executive', then that manager can only manage effectively when his or her team have regard for the manager's active power over and above his or her overt power. And within that sales team there will be an informal hierarchy and power structure, which it is important for the manager to understand.

RAISING YOUR POWER

We may build active power at work through:

- *Reputation and track record*
  Often people's achievements become mythologised and exaggerated. If a manager joins a sales team from another department

where he or she enjoyed a good reputation, this will go before them and influence the attitude of the team.

Our regard for reputation is often irrational. In the way that military tactics fail by being repeated without regard to changed environment and situation, we expect people to live up to their reputation when the circumstances in which they are performing are very different. It's wise to adapt accordingly.

- *Ability, knowledge and experience*
  'Expert power' is a prized resource these days, when a large percentage of the population appear to be earning their living as 'consultants' of one description or another. We now live in the 'information society', where specialised skills and knowledge are valued. The ideal manager is now regarded as a coach who helps others develop their skills and can act as a role model, rather than as an authoritarian figure issuing orders by virtue of his or her overt status. Performing their job to the best of their ability, such managers set an example for others to follow.

- *Understanding of values*
  Within organisations and even within departments there are values which take priority and create the culture. In the book *Corporate Cultures*, by Terence Deal and Allen Kennedy 'culture' is defined as 'the way things are done around here'. A retail organisation, for instance, may place priority on action, customer service and teamwork. A government department may place emphasis on careful administration and attention to detail, to research and to political manoeuvring. Intellectual prowess may be valued in the research department, whereas persuasion may be the most valued skill in marketing.

- *Making contacts*
  Having access to influential people and people who can give you information is helpful. This isn't the same as being popular or impressing the bosses. A lot of people may like you, but it can be more useful to know a smaller, selective number – like the managing director's secretary, for instance, who's been with the company twenty-five years, and who loves to chat and fill you in on the history.

  In acknowledging other people's active power, by finding out about them and their personal lives through informal socialising regardless of overt power, it's possible to learn and understand a great deal.

- *Using personal attributes*
  In groups, there needs to be a balance of personalities. Research into group dynamics indicates that a group of high achievers, for example, do not perform as well as a mixed-ability group. You may gain status at work from your ability to make everyone laugh and to defuse tense atmospheres, from your informal counselling skills or your ability to see the down-side and to be eminently practical when others are dreaming.

- *Having an overview*
  Consideration of the effects of stress in the workplace has meant that for many employers the workaholic has become bad news. This stressed-out poor performer is motivated by the fear that he or she is highly disposable, and that if they ease up on their workload the axe will fall. But having an overview means giving yourself time for outside interests that you can talk about and that provide recreation for your brain from work.

  Having an overview also means being in the picture about your role and those of your subordinates and superiors in the company, about your company's profile in the larger comparative corporate picture, and keeping up to date with all that's new in your business or profession through professional organisations, the trade press and national newspapers. It's said that information is power – it's also an immensely sensitive barometer to shifting status levels, whatever the weather.

- *Seeing beyond overt power*
  People become self-important to counteract and to attack the fear that they are insignificant. And the self-important make indiscriminate use of the symbols of overt power – the job title, large office, several secretaries – to bolster their malnourished egos. This use may become authoritarian and overpowering for subordinates. They'll jump to your tune, but it's unlikely that they'll hang around to hear the final Act of the opera.

It's useful to be able to see beyond other people's use of overt power, and to remember that the rank difference *only* applies at work. The greatest difficulties are often to do with people who are very close in overt power and who are therefore threatening to one another. Let's return to the example of our sales team, which now has a manager and a chief sales executive. The manager may be wary of the chief sales executive because he or she is the obvious choice to replace the manager, since he or she enjoys high active power with the rest of the team. In return the chief sales executive may be wary of the manager, because he or she seeks higher overt power and the manager is blocking this. He or she may also suspect that the manager has far greater access to a lot of useful information. We often assume that those above us know much more than they do. As described in Chapter Three, the manager may use cryptic messages to reinforce this impression.

> People most strenuously seek to evaluate their performance by comparing themselves to others, not by using absolute standards.
>
> *In Search of Excellence*, Tom Peters

In summary, here are some practical steps to raise your active power:

- 'Leak' your past successes through other people, or disclose them yourself in a suitably modest and reluctant manner, as is the British way.

- Seek training and learning to increase your ability and specialist knowledge. If your company won't pay for it, take responsibility for your own learning. Your long-term goals may make it worth sacrificing your two weeks in Turkey for a training course. Shop around for a recommended one, or ask the training or personnel department for advice.

- View your experience as having provided *adaptable* skills. The woman returner can feel inadequate when she goes back to work, forgetting that she's spent several years managing and developing human resources at home.

- Find an area that interests you, which is small and highly specialised, in which you can build an 'expert' reputation. A highly specialised knowledge of tax law, for instance, may stand you in much better stead than an MBA, when MBAs are becoming increasingly common. And, of course, if your specialist skills are in a growth area so much the better. How to find growth areas? Read the newspapers and trade press.

- Consider the importance of values in terms of culture and job. Would you describe yourself as intellectual, practical, creative, sociable, self-motivated, conforming, individual? Are your needs met to some extent by the culture and job? Does your history limit you in the culture? (In my experience non-graduates, for instance, can find it very difficult to get above a certain level in some companies.)

- Keep your ear to the ground and mix with people from other departments and those who are 'in the know'. Go along to social events and join in extra-curricular activities. In a new job, a few quick drinks after work can provide you with a great deal of information and understanding. But social conditioning can make this more difficult for women. To avoid the risk of misinterpretation, state your intention clearly: 'John, can I buy you lunch/a drink after work? I'd like your advice on how the company works.'

- Be open and accessible. Revealing information about yourself and your family will foster trust in others and encourage them to entrust you with their confidences. Don't try to be infallible, godlike or always on your best behaviour: it's extremely stressful. If you tell a good story in the pub, use this ability when appropriate to entertain at work (during presentations, for instance. Some people, though, use humour constantly to avoid issues – see Chapter Three – and someone who does this will end up being regarded as class buffoon.) Let people know who you are, warts and all.

- Maintain an overview on your job and your personal goals, and regularly appraise progress. Is it taking you in the right direction? Some people leave it very late to discover that they may not be aggressive/intellectual/pragmatic enough to succeed in their particular company. Or perhaps values have changed since they first joined. You may not want to go further in your job – perhaps the status you have in your social and personal life may prove sufficient.

Here are some questions that may help you further define the values of your department and/or organisation:

- Is the emphasis on team players or are there mavericks (nonconformists) and stars in the company?

- Is the hierarchy clearly defined? With many levels? Are senior people accessible or remote?

- Are there predominant characteristics among senior people/stars? (They may be almost entirely male, from a certain class/background, super salespeople, conservative, outgoing etc.)

- Is there much emphasis on training, and if so is it based on action 'Learn as you do' or the more traditional 'Talk and chalk'? (Some company cultures have 'nurture' as an important value, while others regard training as a dangerous activity which results in rapid staff turnover.)

- How risky in terms of money/reputation is the job you do for the company? How big are the risks, and how often do you take them?

- Do you get results quickly and often, or do they take a long time to come through? What expectations are placed on quantity compared to quality of work that you do?

- Do you need to think big or to pay a lot of attention to detail?

- Are you required to be persistent at repeating the same task many times (phoning sales prospects, for instance) or persistent in seeing a long, slow project through to the end (overseeing a two-year training programme, for instance)?

- Is there much competition between people at work, or are you united in fighting external competition?

- Does the organisation foster a sense of belonging and membership through organised social events, sports and recreation facilities, and 'perks' to employees?

- What does the environment you work in say about the company and its attitude towards employees?

THE TRAPPINGS OF OVERT POWER

She took the lift to the fifteenth floor. The managing director's secretary led her to his office through two ante-rooms. Her feet sank into the thick pile of the carpet. She walked into a spacious room on the corner of the building, with large windows on two sides providing panoramic views of the City. His large walnut desk was at one end, at the other were plush leather chairs with an expensive glass coffee table. There was very little clutter in the room; one bold modern painting on the wall. The air conditioning was on high, the room cool and silent, the atmosphere controlled and rarified. . . .

Size and location of office, level of distraction, quality of decor and furniture and fittings can all be signs of overt power. In some companies rank is measured in terms of floor space, and the most sought-after offices are those with large window space. High power is indicated through inaccessibility, human and physical barriers keeping the rank and file at a distance. Phone calls are thoroughly screened; people have to make appointments a long time in advance. Someone who has a lot of overt power has a great deal to do: their time and attention are very precious.

Extensive space and limited time show overt power. Your mode of transport is important too. The managing director may travel in a chauffeur-driven Jaguar, the pop star in a stretch limo with blacked out windows so as to preserve distance. For many of us, though, it's more likely to be the size and model of our company car and the allocation of a reserved parking space that acts as an advert for our status.

SHIFTING STATUS

The status we enjoy is relative to the group we are in. The managing director who enjoys high status of both types will have to shift his roles and expectations when he's asked by the rest of the board to answer criticism of company performance. The manager who is given status by her sales team largely due to her expert power will have to adjust her role when she meets informally with a group of other managers from different departments. In either case, inability to shift status through behaviour and attitude would alienate others. Inability to shift status when moving from workplace to home can also cause difficulties.

Since many people derive a strong sense of status from the recognition they get at work, when they stop working they need to readjust. Relocation counsellors – occupational psychologists who are paid by companies to see their senior executives through periods of redundancy – recognise this. The counsellors may provide displaced executives with 'mini-offices' – their own office space and secretarial back-up that can be used on a daily basis. The executives, though stripped of job title status, keep some sense of territorial status. And they are able to tell headhunters and prospective employers that they are working from a serviced office in town.

When people stop working through redundancy, retirement or maternity they need to find other ways of getting their needs fulfilled. Hobbies, learning, the new role itself, more available time to spend with family and friends may effectively do this.

As a newcomer to a job and organisation, you may find yourself groping around to discover how status operates. Like this fifty-year-old ex-army major now employed in industry:

> When I left the army a couple of years ago, I had great difficulty coming to terms with my change in status. In the army you know what's what, who's above you and below you, so to speak, and that status is authority-based. In industry I found the status system much more difficult to comprehend. It was far less overt. In my first few months I made some real gaffes – sitting in the wrong part of the dining room, for instance, and using a commanding manner with staff who weren't used to it. I have found much more concern with status in industry than I expected – it's just not so easy to identify for a newcomer. When people move from the armed forces into civilian life, they often need to make considerable adjustment to the way status operates.

If you choose to dispense with conventional displays of overt status, bear in mind how conformist, conservative and resistant to change many people are. The managing director who suddenly assumes a very friendly, familiar manner may be regarded with suspicion; the accountant who turns up to work in his track suit may be ridiculed. Non-conformists are often regarded as mad, bad and dangerous to know. When playing status games, remember the status quo.

Competition

There is a limited amount of overt status to go round, and it is defined by its exclusivity. Only a small number of the company can have Jaguar cars, for instance. This makes some people over-concerned and competitive about it. As active status is so specific to the individual and based on experience, specialist knowledge, awareness, ability and social skills there is far less need to compete for it. You get on and do your own thing, and respect others who do the same.

COMMUNICATING POWER

For others to regard you as having power, you have to be able to communicate it. Your impressive track record on paper must be matched by your ability to talk about it, otherwise you will lose credibility. In this next section we'll examine how power games are played in interviews, meetings and presentations and on the telephone.

Much of the interaction in these situations is to do with persuasion. An interviewer may want to persuade an interviewee to join their company; the main objective of a presentation may be to persuade your audience to buy a service you are selling. Later on I'll consider persuasion in greater detail. At this point it's worth mentioning that one of the best approaches to persuasion in any situation can be to ask yourself: 'What's in it for them?' and to consider what needs (as mentioned earlier in this chapter) you can meet.

Interviews

Interviews are fraught with status interactions because of their very nature: meetings with a purpose, and that purpose being the assessment of one person by another. This goes for job interviews, appraisal interviews and disciplinary interviews.

Job Interviews

'I think it's a waste of time holding interviews. But someone's got to do it, so here I am. Shall we start?' Senior partner in law firm, to young graduate on his first interview (sub-text: 'I really don't want to be here, wasting my time talking to you').

With the forecast demographic changes, companies are now starting to take greater care over the impression an interviewer makes. After all, he or she is the siren who can lure the young graduate or woman returner into their particular workplace. The role is a responsible one; an interviewer who makes a bad mistake could cost the company a lot of money.

Interviewees may be over-suspicious of the interviewer, waiting to be trapped, and they may read too much into what the interviewer says and does. Sensing this, the unskilled or inexperienced interviewer may attempt to raise his or her overt power by playing any one of a number of roles:

- *The judge*
  Uses behaviour that emphasises the interviewer's powers to appraise and evaluate – sitting back in the chair, head tilting backwards, hand covering mouth, perhaps, looking doubtful and not registering any reaction to what is said, or indicating that he or she appreciates that their 'victim' has finished an answer. No encouragement is given to the interviewee. The judge may ask open, vague questions, affording the interviewee plenty of rope to hang himself or herself; for instance, 'Tell me all about yourself', which means, of course, 'Tell me specific information about yourself that makes you right for this job.'

- *The big-shot*
  Resorts to ridiculous tactics like sitting the interviewee on a small, armless chair opposite a window so that he or she is blinking in a stream of sunlight. The Obergruppenführer, meanwhile, is sitting on a large leather revolving chair behind a vast expanse of desk. The office is filled with awards, certificates, personal and company memorabilia. This is a corporate warrior's office, and the interviewee's going to be left in no doubt about it. Midway through the interview the big-shot deliberately looks at his or her ostentatious watch. The big-shot's unlikely to leave time for the interviewee to ask questions at the end.

- *The interrogator*
  This interviewer sees himself or herself as the natural successor to Jeremy Paxman. They'll justify their behaviour by saying that the interviewee needs to perform well under pressure to do the job.

They'll ask two-part questions: 'What made you leave then, and why did you choose to move to – ?': leading questions: 'The company was in a terrible mess then – what part do you think your department played?'; and 'why?' questions which require justification and can be asked ad infinitum:

'Why did you change jobs then?'

'I wanted more of a challenge.'

'Why?'

'I wasn't realising my potential.'

'Why?' . . . and so on. If this type of interviewer senses a weak spot he or she will hang on in there – mercilessly.

- *The creep*
  The insecurity that the interviewer experiences may cause them to smile manically; to talk too much, when he or she should be able to take responsibility for pauses; to do a really hard sell on behalf of the company; to over-react with approval to the interviewee, giving them, unfairly, the impression that they've got the job. The creep will also say things like, 'Oh, I know just how you feel' or 'I hear what you say', and by the end of the interview you'll know as much about them as they know about you.

The interviewer is expected to take control. Insensitive interviewers are often influenced too much by their personal prejudices to an interviewee and fail to appreciate the interviewee's nervousness. Like interviewees, interviewers can learn skills which mean they don't have to resort to overt power games (which the discriminating interviewee will see through). These skills include:

- *Helping the interviewee relax*
  Through easy small talk at the beginning and by humour, giving a relaxed impression themselves.

- *Stopping the interviewee talking too much*
  Through using eye contact and body language to indicate that it's time to move on. Through asking closed questions requiring 'yes', 'no' or one-word answers, and by stipulating 'I'd like to move on to. . . .' Interruptions work, too.

- *Getting the interviewee to talk more*
  Through nodding and sending encouraging listening signals. Through slowing down the pace and using plenty of pause.

Through asking open questions requiring longer answers: 'how' questions are especially useful. 'How did you think that went?', for instance.

- *Stopping the interviewee waffling*
  Through asking definite questions asking for concrete detail. For example, 'How many products did you develop there?', 'What percentage of your time did you spend travelling?'

- *Easing the interviewee's discomfort*
  Through moving on to questions which invite rational, positive answers when the interviewee seems 'thrown' or upset.

The interviewee, on the other hand, may lower his or her power by playing the following roles:

- *The victim*
  Uses low-status behaviour, avoids eye contact, keeps the face frozen, uses defensive body language, mumbles, speaks too quickly or too quietly, and uses too many 'ums' and 'ers'. Victims use lots of apology and paint themselves as mundane and inadequate in what they say. To the interviewer, the victim looks like a frightened rabbit who can't wait to get back into the warren.

  The victim can raise his or her status through standing and sitting tall and proud, making steady eye contact with the interviewer from the outset, taking time to answer questions and responding in a clear voice. Unlike a real victim, the interview underdog needs to remember that he or she is also in a position to evaluate. Your interviewer is a representative of the organisation and you are judging them as such. If you don't like your reception, it could be their loss.

- *The chatterbox*
  Talks incessantly to the point of forgetting what the original question was, using long, rambling sentences which go on for so long that the interviewee can't remember where they started. When asked 'What did you like about your last job?' the chatterbox's reply includes a detailed description of her recent holiday in the Dordogne. The chatterbox will keep talking about anything so long as there isn't a pause where there could be an opportunity to engage brain before mouth.

  Chatterboxes need to listen, to use short, succinct sentences, to wait and think before replying, and to check that their answers are relevant to the questions. Rehearsing the likely interview with a friend and asking them to look out for these points can help.

- *The philosopher*
Doesn't like being put on the spot and adopts conceptualising and abstract thinking to counter this. So, for instance, when asked: 'What has been your greatest achievement?' the philosopher's reply will start with 'Well, it depends what you really mean by "greatest achievement" and the context in which you're using it.' The reply will continue with ramblings on 'the true meaning of "great" and "achieve" and the likelihood of absolute truth'. All this is done while the philosopher stares abstractedly out of the window and the interviewer dozes off.

  Philosophers can come across as overbearingly pompous. They frustrate the interviewer who wants to know specific tangible facts about the past to assess how this information could be utilised in the future. Philosophers need to stop procrastinating and staring at their navels and answer questions like the one above with a definite answer. For instance: 'My greatest achievement so far has been supervising the Brillo campaign.'

- *The braggart*
Is very insecure and boasts – as much to tell themselves that they are important as to tell the interviewer. The braggart turns every question into an answer that makes himself or herself look incredibly good. So when asked about 'greatest achievements' the braggart will have so many that the interviewer will get earache. Braggarts talk *at* the interviewer and are often so concerned and anxious about themselves that they fail to notice how the interviewer is responding.

  Braggarts can help themselves by working on responding to signals that other people use, looking and listening. In preparation for the interview, the braggart should think of all the uncomfortable, difficult questions he or she might be asked and set about preparing honest answers to them. Controlling body language and voice so that they don't convey self-importance also helps. Pointing out the odd negative aspect and down-side to things will also make you appear more rational.

More and more companies are now using *psychometric tests* as back-up to the job interview. These can help interviewers assess personality and give a clearer picture of the interviewee's strengths and weaknesses. The use of these tests can seem threatening to the status of the interviewee, in the sense that hidden secrets are going to be discovered. Three points are worth considering:

- For every strength discovered in a test there is a corresponding weakness.

- Good interviewers do not use these tests as a substitute for interview, merely as an additional aid. When the tests are used fairly the interviewer will have been tested himself or herself, and use the results as an indication of, and insurance against, their own prejudices.

- In most cases, quite fairly, the interviewer will give you feedback on the test. This can be useful for self-awareness and offer guidance for skills development.

A typical test in its most basic application might help identify the extent to which you use and prefer:

- (a) Socialising, action, variety, experience
  compared to
  solitude, reflection, dedication to a single goal, understanding.

- (b) A realistic, practical approach, attention to detail and facts
  compared to
  a creative, imaginative approach, concerned with vision and potential.

- (c) Analysis, logic, thought processes, discussion
  compared to
  empathy, rapport, emotions, agreement.

- (d) Decision-making, determination, resolution, organisation
  compared to
  enquiry, toleration, open-endedness, spread of input.

It can be useful to ask yourself whether the profile that emerges is one that suits the job you are applying for.

Appraisal and Disciplinary Interviews

As an interviewee in these situations, you can maintain your power by:

- Asking for clarification of any points that you do not understand.

- Getting information about your strengths as well as your weaknesses.

- Being absolutely clear what targets you are being set, what your performance is expected to be and how it will be assessed.

- Doing a pre-interview evaluation yourself of how your past performance has matched targets, and determining your reasons for success and failure.

- Asking for further training if necessary, a change in job definition or conditions, and for information about any future changes that may affect your objectives.

PERSUADING PEOPLE: MEETINGS AND PRESENTATIONS

It's said that 'everyone sells'. Much of the communication we do at work is concerned with building personal integrity and credibility, with getting other people to accept opinions and advice and then to act on it. Lots of time and money is wasted through inadequate consideration and understanding of persuasion techniques. Telephone sales teams daily insult the intelligence of thousands of potential customers, as they read at them from a prepared sales script. In telephone and face-to-face selling standard sales pitches are used, regardless of the specific needs of the customer. The salesperson fails to give the customer recognition as an individual, so the customer's status is diminished. It's hardly surprising that in retaliation many people regard the pushy salesperson with contempt.

Of course, persuasion is not just confined to selling. When we offer advice, seek support for our ideas or seek to gain commitment to a course of action we are attempting to persuade. We do it all the time.

Step one, then, in intelligent persuasion is to acknowledge the status of your 'audience' through targeting what you say and how you say it to meet the specific needs of the individuals involved: the 'What's in it for you?' factor. Don't assume that your 'audience' thinks like you do. Familiarity with the case, product or service you are discussing may make you blinkered. You may think that the advantages and benefits on offer are glaringly obvious – so obvious, in fact, that you don't need to express them. Check that everyone is aware of what they are and how they are pertinent to the individuals involved. And the most vital step in preparing to persuade is to find out as much as you can about the people you are targeting. Political parties spend vast amounts of money finding out who their supporters and detractors are and what their views are on key issues.

Here's one method of identifying persuasion 'triggers' (there are lots of others). Ask yourself:

(a) Whom am I attempting to persuade? Draw up as detailed a picture as possible.

(b) Can I appeal to:

- *Psychological needs*

  Some of us give to charity because it appeases our guilt. We may succumb to flattery because it makes us feel good. A strong intellectual or emotional appeal may reinforce self-image; the appeal bolsters up my idea of myself as a rational/analytical/thinking person or as a warm/empathetic/sensitive one. Too one-sided a pitch, appealing exclusively to intellect or emotions, is unlikely to be effective.

  Without scruple politicians use fear as a persuasion weapon, targeting psychological needs: 'If you don't vote for us you will lose freedom of choice/risk maltreatment under the NHS/deprive your children of good education/lessen the chance of losing the roof over your head.' In particular, fear is used to threaten security. Insurance salespeople can use similar tactics. Perhaps one of the reasons why politicians as a breed are such unpopular people is because of the indiscriminate use of threats to meet their own objectives.

  'It's always been done this way' is one of the biggest hurdles to overcome when persuading others. We are creatures of habit, and we are suspicious of change and the unknown. So if I make the ecologically sound washing powder Ecover and I want you to buy it instead of your familiar Persil, I need to change your habit.

A most effective means of doing this is through flattery and giving you the status of an innovative thinker. If I remind you that you are a person who is aware, receptive to new ideas and willing to give them a try, then my suggestion that you buy Ecover is likely to be well received.

- *Peer group pressure*
  This influence meets psychological needs in that we most of us crave acceptability – we seek to identify with groups to make sense of our world, and we aspire to join other groups. We live in a time when television tells us what our world is like and what lifestyles other people have and we can copy. Most advertising applies a lot of peer group pressure: if you are the successful executive you're trying to be, you must fly British Airways rather than the red-eye. If you're the concerned young mother, you must give your baby 'natural' (whatever that is) food.

  Peer group pressure is also effective when selling ideas. 'Our business rivals are thinking like this, so why don't we?', 'All the departments who are successful in this company have used these methods, so why don't we?', 'If we want to be up there with the big boys then let's study and use their tactics.'

  Trend prediction is now big business to help commerce and industry keep up with the latest demands created by peer group pressure.

- *Material gain*
  We allow ourselves to be persuaded when we think we are going to get richer, to have a more luxurious lifestyle, to make acquisitions. Some of us are very keen to raise our outward show of status.

- *Spirit of enquiry*
  Lately, 'teasers' have become popular copy in advertising. Teasers are copylines or images that do not mention the service or product, but whet your appetite to discover more. For instance, when Billy Graham visited Britain in 1990, several weeks before he arrived there were posters all over London with the initials L.I.F.E. – what was it? When he arrived the riddle was answered through posters announcing his presence.

  In using this trigger you again reinforce status and self-image. We have to assume that, if someone wants to explore a concept or examine an idea, he or she has an intelligent, enquiring mind.

- *Physical needs*
  Politicians have been persuaded to divulge secrets through sex. Physical gratification often plays a contributing role in the exercise of persuasion: what does the marketing manager expect in return for the expensive lunch she's buying you? Is that fine food and wine going to affect your judgement and make you easier to persuade?

To sum up, then, when planning to persuade ask yourself the following:

- Whom am I persuading, and what are their various needs and values?

- How can I acknowledge their status? Are there assumptions I can safely make about the language they understand, their level of awareness, the social and political groups they identify with?

- Can I make them feel good about themselves/reinforce their self-image? Am I comfortable using flattery, guilt and fear as persuasion triggers?

- How do I appeal to their intellect (language, facts and figures, concepts), and what emotions am I stimulating?

- What peer group pressure can I apply?

- Am I going to play on their curiosity?

- Am I offering the possibility of making money?

Meetings

Meetings provide good opportunities to practise persuasion and to raise your power among subordinates, peers and bosses. Here are some ways of doing this:

Preparing in Advance

On a course I was running, one of the exercises was to role play a meeting on the sensitive subject of company cars. When the exercise was explained, one of the participants piped up with 'But we don't meet beforehand?' In that particular company that was essential pre-meeting preparation. You sought out your supporters, briefed them beforehand, then went into the meeting knowing you had strength in numbers. In some organisations, like government for instance, pre-meeting lobbying is the expected norm. When this is the case, pre-meeting briefing of supporters to get them to ask the right questions (ones that you can answer well) and to bring in relevant information and viewpoints is essential.

Be clear about the purpose of the meeting and the case you are to present, and that your attendance is necessary. Your case may be strengthened by preparing written material to back up what you say. If an agenda is being prepared, try and get your item dealt with early on. Check that you know who else is to be present, anticipate what 'hidden agendas' they may have and be sure that you know the level of formality. Decisions are often reached more quickly when a chairperson is doing their role effectively and pulling strands together than when opinions are being tossed haphazardly around a group.

Checking Procedure

Meetings are often held because 'that's the way things are done around here'. Although meetings are not always called to decide upon definite action – the purpose may be, for instance, to do a 'raincheck' on the progress of a project – everyone involved should have a clear idea of the meeting's objective(s) and an active contribution to make. Sometimes the issue may be dealt with more effectively via memos and telephone calls.

If the start is disorganised, then lead the way. Ask whether a chairperson is necessary, what items there are for the agenda and how timing is to be arranged. If there's no one present who's been designated as minute-taker, then avoid volunteering – especially if you were once a secretary. The minute-taker will find it difficult to make an active vocal contribution. Taking note of every small detail that occurs makes it impossible to take part in active discussion.

Avoid being preoccupied with procedure; once the shape of the meeting has been defined you want to move on with your contribution, while being sure that the focus remains clear. Some people become 'procedure police' at meetings; they dodge joining in discussion of matters under consideration by constantly raising 'points of order'. This is perhaps the only way they feel they can be effective in the situation.

Checking procedure can be used tactically to support your

purpose. If your item of concern has been placed at the end of the agenda, the probability is that time will run out and you may want to get it moved forward. When you haven't had time to prepare, however, you may want to leave the item just where it is. If limited time has been allocated to deal with an item, and your case is not succeeding, you can point out that time has run out as a diversionary tactic. When you need to put pressure on someone, reminding them of time limits can increase their stress level and make them capitulate sooner rather than later. A visit or television viewing of the House of Commons is recommended to anyone wanting to watch all these ploys and many more in action.

Getting in Early

'I go to a meeting, have some really good points to make, but because I get paralysed about speaking out I remain silent. Afterwards, I could kick myself.' The quantity and quality of your contribution matter if you're to gain attention. If you play the role of the insignificant bystander, then your status will fall. You need to behave as though you are worthy of, and deserve, recognition.

Acknowledge people when you arrive rather than slinking into a corner. If people are chatting before the formal start of the meeting, then get involved in conversation – it will warm you up. Once the meeting starts, make a contribution early. If you are new to a company, lower in overt power than the rest of the people present or simply shy, the easiest contribution to make is to ask a question. In asking for clarification, information or advice, you ask the rest of the meeting to help you and no one can think of that as presumptuous. Set yourself a time limit if it helps: 'I must ask a question in the first five minutes.' Once you've made your initial contribution it's much easier to continue. If necessary and you're a skilled enough actor (and most of us are), invent something to clarify: 'I'm not quite sure what item three means – can anybody explain to me please?' The main thing is to get in early.

Concentrated Listening

In Chapter Three I described how we disguise our motives in conversation through using sub-text. By giving concentrated attention to others you can improve your skills at identifying other people's subtext and motives. Concentrated listening involves focusing on tone of voice, facial expression and body language as well as the words used. Poor listeners often make irrelevant comments; the most influential contributions do not necessarily come from those vessels making the most noise.

You can exert considerable control in a meeting through concentrated listening and then making a relevant contribution. You can offer analysis, interpretation, solutions and suggestions. While you maintain involvement in terms of your behaviour, you can think about especially pertinent questions that need answering and use them to clarify or challenge. Take time to work out who are allies in the meeting and, if you have a case to argue, who are the most influential people present. In America, some law firms use consultants to analyse the behaviour of jury members and to choose the main 'influencers' among them; the attorney then pitches his or her case to those people.

Voicing Your Opinions

Don't shy away from saying what you think. Taking a friend aside and sharing your views afterwards may be safer, but it won't raise your power. Use short sentences to make your points clearly. If you can see puzzled faces, ask people whether you've expressed your message clearly enough. You may need to amplify (especially if you possess expert knowledge about something).

Express your support for others and let people know when you agree or disagree, giving reasons why. When another person indicates support for something you have said, build on that alliance by acknowledging their contribution: 'Bill's made a very good point there', and, if appropriate, back them up ('and what I think is also relevant' or 'I'd like to add to what he said by . . .'). That way you build strength in numbers. When you're keen to push something through, summarise at regular intervals: 'So are we at the point where we've got agreement over this?' or 'Can I ask if we all accept that more money is needed?'

When you are directly opposed by another person who is launching a strong attack, it can be useful to:

● Write notes on what they say, suggesting that a record is being kept (this can help you think more rationally about counter-attack, but it may be distracting – in which case, a supporter could do it).

- Ask for reasons and justification for what they are saying, using 'why' questions. Apply gentle pressure to make them appear more extreme. By contrast you will appear all the more reasonable.

- Refuse to get diverted, and keep using the 'broken record' technique of repeating your case (see p. 31).

- Keep your behaviour calm and reasonable, and maintain your sense of humour if possible. 'Zooming out' of what's going on and commenting on it, without apportioning blame, may help defuse tension: 'Things seem to be getting a little heated at the moment.' Remind yourself that your attacker may have poor communication skills – their aggression may be the only way they are able to express themselves.

- Ignore personal attacks and criticism by thanking the opposition for their feedback and then moving on with the positive aspects of your case. Avoid justifying or defending the criticism too much, or you will look defensive. Many of us find this very difficult. Keep calm, and resist the temptation to launch a personal attack back. That is deflecting from your main purpose of persuading most of the people present to accept your case.

- Compliment the opposition. You are threatening them, and they may be disarmed by compliments. For instance 'I think Bill's put his case exceptionally well' or 'We all know Bill is a great authority on this.' Think about the opposition's needs when you do this.

- Remember that you want to influence the group, not just win a two-way battle. When the interchange starts to get heated, ask the rest of the meeting for their views. Keep taking the temperature of the meeting. And whatever the outcome, victory or defeat, leave obvious displays of gloating, anger or tears until afterwards.

When everyone is speaking at once in a meeting, keep talking in a calm, reasonable manner. You will get through eventually. Despite your conditioning (women tend to have greater difficulty doing this than men), interrupt if necessary and state your intention. 'Can I interrupt, please?' Humour can work here, too: 'Hello, hello! Am I really so insignificant that nobody will listen to me?'

Encouraging Others

Your use of language and syntax is important. It's easier to get your case accepted if you offer it as a collective decision: 'Something we could consider is. . .', 'Shall we go for that. . .?' rather than 'I think we must . . .' or 'I insist we. . .'. When everyone present feels involved in the decision, their commitment to it will be much stronger. You can maintain 'official ownership' of your case by summarising for the minutes ('Following my proposal the meeting agreed. . .') and by literally having the last word on the item: 'So we're agreed on that. Shall we move on?'

You can also foster a sense of 'collectiveness' by turning suggestions and proposals into questions. 'I suggest we review next year's budget and make some radical changes. What does everybody think?' When someone's silent for a long time, ask them for an opinion. They may be quietly simmering over something they feel very strongly about.

If someone is present who doesn't enjoy speaking or is prominent through being an outsider, on a much lower level, or even a different gender from everyone else, make sure they get included. When this person makes a short, stilted contribution encourage the speaker through obviously listening and asking them to continue: 'What else do you think about the proposal?' or 'Can I ask Bill to say some more about his department?'

Someone who is good at abstract thinking and conceptualising may hold up proceedings and appear to be talking in a void, away from everyone else. Putting a practical question to them: 'So what action should those ideas lead us to take, do you think?' can make their contribution that much more relevant.

Sitting in the Best Position

This is largely a matter of common sense. When the meeting has a chair who will exert strong control, put yourself clearly in his or her line of vision. Sitting with your allies will help strengthen your sense of solidarity. If you sit directly opposite an opponent, the sense of conflict may be heightened. Sitting at right-angles to them (on either side of the corner of a table) or even alongside them will make for more harmony.

Seating depends on room arrangement and table size; but the more in the centre you are of any line the better your range of vision, and the better placed you are to get involved. Stake out plenty of territory, always a high-status activity, by spreading your papers in front of you and using expansive body language (especially if you are physically small, or female). Keep your posture upright and relaxed; it will help you maintain a high level of energy.

In meetings people may lessen their power through:

- Remaining disinterested and uninvolved, thereby creating distance. They may think this is high-status play because nobody knows what they're thinking. The trouble is nobody ends up caring, either.

- Aggression, personal attacks and criticism, behaving like a petulant child.

- Not listening, and talking too much about irrelevancies. This reveals how insecure they are and how threatened they feel by other people's opinions.

- Disagreeing with everything and everyone. This can be a method that some people use to assert themselves. Their self-image tells them that they are 'controversial', so they act this out.

Presentations

These situations offer an even better opportunity to raise your status than meetings. If things go smoothly you've got the attention of a captive audience, you exert far greater control over events than in a meeting, and you are developing skills which are invaluable in gaining prominence. In most organisations there are few people who enjoy reputations as good presenters, even at a senior level. And if you build a reputation as such by making internal presentations this can lead to promotion to a position where you become an ambassador, making external ones to clients, customers and new business. Looking comfortable centre stage can be the first step to getting your name up in lights.

You can help your presentations raise your power in a number of ways:

Giving Your Audience Status
The starting point for planning your presentation should be recognition of the particular needs of your audience, along with your own needs and an analysis of how they match up.

The starting point for delivering your presentation should be physically to recognise them – that is, to look at them. Otherwise, you may find that they are not what you had anticipated and you may need to adapt your performance. When you look at your audience you show consideration of them and their responses.

Lack of presentation is an insult to the audience. Let them know that you haven't prepared, and you insult them even further. You also diminish their status when you tell them how to react: 'I'm sorry, this is going to be boring – but here goes' or 'I'm going to tell you a very funny story now.' You can also instruct them how to react through your own behaviour: shrugging your shoulders apologetically at the end of your presentation says, 'Go on, regard me with contempt.'

You compliment your audience when you consider their capacity for discrimination. When your audience are bombarded with lots of words on dozens of overheads which you helpfully read aloud, you're not doing this. You're spelling everything out for them, 'cos the poor dears aren't very bright, are they?

Acknowledge your audience's status through using language they can understand, and ideas they can identify with. To indicate that they matter ask them questions, entertain them, encourage them to respond. When appropriate to your content, acknowledge the active status of individuals present. So when you're talking about marketing and the marketing manager's in the audience, you could say, 'Whoops, I'm on dangerous ground – I know John over there knows a lot more about this than I do.'

Elevate the status of your audience through assuming they know more than they do but explaining it anyway. For example, if you're talking about marketing again, to the same audience with John the marketing manager and his department present, you could say: 'I'm going to talk a little about the marketing concept. All of you know something about it, I'm sure. John and his team are more than familiar with it but it is important, so please bear with me while I spell it out.' In this instance, John and his buddies will be happy that their 'expert knowledge' and power has been publicly recognised, and the bulk of the audience who know nothing about the marketing concept are flattered that someone thinks they know something about it.

Handling High Power in the Audience

I don't mind presenting to people I don't know or to the people
I work with. It's presenting to my superiors that I find really
scary. I feel like a naughty schoolkid who's standing in front of
the headmaster.

Head of personnel, advertising agency

Those people who show a strong respect for authority and who
expect negative criticism often dread making presentations to their
superiors (see Chapter Two for more on authority and criticism).
As presenter you have to give much of your attention to your active
involvement in the performance, and so your capacity for evaluation is limited. As an audience member, you can give much of your
attention to evaluation. When you are presenting to high-status
people, who have the power to promote or demote you, you can
feel justifiably vulnerable and exposed. Consider, though, the
following:

- The 'judges' are your superiors only in terms of *overt* power. That
  is, they have an impressive job title. As people, they do not have
  higher *active* power than you do, unless your self-esteem level is
  low. Are you able to identify where this awe comes from?

- It's unlikely that your 'judges' are all excellent presenters. Indeed,
  the probability is (one survey shows that 41 per cent of people
  name speaking in public as their greatest fear) that just under half
  of them do not enjoy presenting.

- Even if they disagree with your content, dissenters will prefer
  your case to be put well. It's much more fun to go into battle with
  someone who's fighting fit than to beat up a victim who's
  languishing after a bout of disastrous presentation. It's unlikely
  that the rest of the audience want to witness a massacre.

- Don't allow yourself to fall victim to self-fulfilling prophecy.
  Dread of the event may mean that you fail to prepare and
  rehearse adequately. Be as tactical as you can, expect to do your
  best, and rehearse in front of allies who are constructively
  critical.

- Your behaviour is extremely important in that it conveys your
  attitude much more effectively and directly than the words you

use. Use high-status non-verbal signals, voice control and appearance signals (see Chapter Seven). Often, an audience member who is insecure about his or her power (and they may enjoy high overt power) will demonstrate the need to get that power acknowledged. They may do this through looking disinterested or scornful, blatantly not listening, interrupting, asking difficult questions and going on the attack. In which case, give the little child what he or she wants – attention. Up your eye contact early in the presentation, so you make the status-player feel important. Make them feel that their response matters to you, which is what they need.

This tactic goes against many of our instincts; when confronted with a difficult audience member, we may tend to ignore the person in the vain hope that he or she will go away. Unfortunately, this rarely happens: the child keeps screaming until he or she gets attention.

The Head Chef Making the Hors d'Oeuvres Approach

In other words, you are leader, and you are offering your audience a 'taster' of what you have on offer. Irrespective of the power of your audience, as presenter you need to lead. You can do this through controlling the environment: 'Can everyone see/hear me?', 'Do we have enough air?'; through controlling proceedings: 'I'll be talking for ten minutes, with five minutes for questions at the end'; and through acting as guide to the presentation, by commenting on the route, 'So that's my second point. My final point is . . .'.

Be selective about what you present. You are whetting your audience's appetite to do business with you, to stimulate their interest and to ask questions. Keep your content clear and direct, garnishing it with anecdotes, examples and case histories. Make a small number of clear points. Err towards brevity: you want to leave people wanting more, so that they ask questions.

Whatever the response to your presentation, keep control as leader during question time. People often ask questions to bolster your power as presenter or to bolster their own power in the audience. Your supporters will ask questions that you can answer skilfully (you may want to plant these). Your detractors will ask challenging questions or make speeches that they try to disguise as questions. Remember to maintain composure in your behaviour, and to answer questions succinctly. If someone persists in being awkward, then as leader you can choose to continue the discussion with them elsewhere and move on to another questioner. When no one asks any questions, ask the audience for their views on what you've said. At the end of the question period, refocus attention on yourself through repeating your main points, wishing everyone well and thanking them for their attention. As it will be the best remembered part of your presentation, your parting shot needs to be powerful.

THE TELEPHONE

All sorts of power games are played via the telephone. When London phone numbers were divided into 071 for inner London and 081 for outer districts, some people worried that 081 numbers would lower their 'social standing'. More directly, we can play high status on the phone through:

- Being inaccessible. Employing one or several people to answer calls, so that they are screened for their relevance. Leaving the answerphone on, so that you can choose whom to speak to.

- Being 'terribly busy'. The status sub-text here is 'I have little time to talk to you' or 'I'm a person who is very much in demand.' With such value placed on professional success these days, even very close friends may find it necessary (whether true or not) to indicate that they are 'very busy'.

- Not returning calls, or taking a long time to do so. The status sub-text here is 'You are not important' or 'You're a low priority.' The extremely important very busy type may ask if they can call you back – and then forget to do so.

- Keeping people talking on the phone. Telephone sales people use this tactic. They keep you talking by asking questions in order to attempt to engage your interest in whatever they are selling. Many of us are too polite to resist their pressure and we end up sacrificing our time to their sales pitch. Other people may keep talking at you as a means of reinforcing their relationship to you: 'I matter to you, so you must give me plenty of airtime.'

- Being over-brusque. Status sub-text: 'I'm too busy for anything as insignificant as exchanging pleasantries, so let's get 'on with it'.

- Sounding bored, aggressive, self-important. It's extraordinary how many businesses man their front lines with speaking voices that fail to give the customer or client any sense of status (see Chapter Seven). The sub-text is often: 'I've no desire whatsoever to be speaking on this phone to anyone.'

To counteract high-status games on the telephone:

- Be persistent and polite. Call the inaccessible first thing in the morning or last thing in the evening, when their 'oppos' may not be there. If this fails, try another means of communication – a polite letter or fax – and then phone.

- Ask the human barricades for advice and help. Acknowledge their status, and they may let you know when the person you want to talk to is available.

- Be aware that people have different attitudes to the phone. Some regard it purely as a means of conveying information, while others regard it as a means of building and maintaining relationships. Become adaptable, so that you can come to the point quickly or ease in to conversation through some social chit-chat, as appropriate.

- If you're confronted on the phone by someone you'd rather not speak to, or asked to name a price or give information you're not ready to give, then always ask if you can call back later. Succinct, direct messages ('I have to go now, I'm sorry') need not sound dismissive if your tone of voice is warm and relaxed.

- Titles can become especially important on the phone. For instance, calling up and asking, 'Can I speak to Bill – um, Bill Jenkins' may lead a PA to believe that you're a close friend of his. Dropping off surnames indicates familiarity. When you get through to him and say, 'Is that Bill Jenkins?' and he replies 'Yes, this is Mr Jenkins', his use of title indicates distance and formality. He is rebuffing your familiarity. With some people it pays to be deferential and to use a title until told otherwise.

Circumstances may be such that you find it difficult to get your needs for personal power met at work. Perhaps you work part-time, or are self-employed and work alone. In Chapter Five I'll consider how you can raise your visibility, whether it's at work, as an entrepreneur or in your community.

chapter five

INCREASING YOUR VISIBILITY

This chapter considers how to use your personal power through increasing your visibility. You will find it relevant if you want to:

- Raise your professional profile, so that more people know who you are and what you do.
- Get publicity for yourself, your business, an organisation, association or cause with which you are connected.

HIGH VISIBILITY

'We know exactly what to ask for. We know exactly how much Paul Gascoigne is worth.'

Mel Stein, Gazza's lawyer

Paul Gascoigne, the England footballer, cried during a match in the 1990 World Cup. His nickname, 'Gazza', had already been legally registered before the tournament. After it, Gazza and his adviser earned a great deal of money from Gazza toiletries, Gazza computer games, Gazza table football, Gazza bedlinen and Gazza exclusives in the *Sun*. Gazza was also available for personal appearances and he even recorded an album.

Gazza has footballing talent and a likeable personality, though a former England team manager described him as 'daft as a brush'. In the summer of 1990 in Britain very few people could ignore Gazza. He was everywhere.

However, as Gazza, the Princess of Wales and Paula Yates have discovered, the fickle media can build you up and then suddenly knock you down again.

Only a minority of us seek Gazza-style fame, given the invasion of privacy and scrutiny of personal life that it involves. With the explosive growth of print and broadcast media, whose daily bread is 'people stories', far more of us have access to these channels to promote ourselves, our businesses and the causes which we champion.

The press and radio and television stations need a constant supply of 'people fodder' to fill their pages and schedules. Private companies and public organisations have become aware of this and the value of the publicity: more and more of them give key personnel media training, so that they make the right impression when they speak to journalists.

If you're aiming at visibility for yourself or something you are associated with, the media is the best way of obtaining it. The Green party, who opted to shun conventional political manoeuvring through the media, found this out to their cost. When they stopped fostering media contacts their support fell dramatically. Later in this chapter there will be practical advice on how to approach the media.

The time is getting near when we will all have the 'fifteen minutes of fame' that Andy Warhol predicted. Here's TV presenter Jonathan Ross in an interview in the *Independent on Sunday*, diminishing the worth of celebrity (a clever tactic this. It makes many of us like him more, the sub-text being: 'What I do is not that important'):

... already it's desperately easy to become a celebrity in this country and if it became any easier, then people wouldn't even be mildly interested. All you have to do is drop your trousers at a function and you can get on a chat show. . . .We've got a kind of odd attitude to fame in this country – a sort of know-ingness on both sides. It's nowhere near as innocent as it was once; no one seriously thinks they've got to idolise you just because you're famous; it's more a big joke.

And there are celebrities whose sole ability appears to be self-promotion. A few years ago, the *Correspondent* newspaper ran a piece headlined 'How Celebrities Cash in on Their Fame'. An imaginary PR company rang around ten agents representing minor celebrities to ask if certain clients would be prepared to open an imaginary supermarket in Surrey. The article compared the responses of the agents to different terms and conditions. The most accommodating celebrity agreed to:

- Open the supermarket for £2000.

- Go into the stocks and be pelted with wet sponges by local schoolchildren.

- Have a candlelit dinner with the managing director of the superstore (for £1000 extra).

- Dress up as a Christmas Elf.

As a measure of the relative value you put on money, celebrity and dignity, you might want to ask yourself whether you would do the same for £3000.

When minor celebrities of the game show presenter ilk can earn £10,000 a day presenting conferences in business, it's clear that the financial rewards for this type of visibility can be very high. The skilful market their visibility and use it to their advantage. Adam Faith for instance went on to become an actor and then a financial consultant to show-business personalities. Edwina Currie, politician brought down by eggs, went on to write books, become a TV personality and newspaper columnist. Whether she cashed in on her celebrity or notoriety depends on your viewpoint.

Visibility, then, is highly marketable. And if you're motivated enough to promote yourself, you don't need to possess extraordinary talent or ability to become a celebrity. And if you have the money, there are public relations companies and image consultants who can help you market yourself or your company to your public. Without celebrities, it's difficult to imagine what our magazines, newspapers and television companies would put in their place.

Many highly visible people tend to play down their self-promotion skills; they were 'just lucky' or 'never wanted to be well known

– it just happened'. It's in their interest to preserve a mystique about how they got where they have. If more people knew how to do it, then established celebrities would be fighting off contenders for their crowns.

To have personal power, your ability and talent need to be visible to others, even if it's just a small, selected group of your peers. Sometimes outstanding ability brings visibility, but this is by no means inevitable. You may be ahead of your time. We just have to consider the writers, scientists, musicians and artists whose achievements have only been recognised posthumously.

People also get high visibility through:

- Leadership ability (John F. Kennedy, Golda Meir, Winston Churchill).

- Marketing their personality (this is what showbusiness and sports celebrity is all about).

- Being born into famous families, marrying into them, or even just consorting with them (the royals, Ivana Trump, Jackie Onassis, Camilla Parker Bowles).

- Representing causes, beliefs, values (Bob Geldof, Emily Pankhurst, David Bellamy, Florence Nightingale).

The skills that go into the marketing of celebrities can be used by all of us and applied to our own concerns. And if you are one of those people who seek fame at any price, it's worth considering tactics like marrying well, creating public controversy and outrage, or committing an especially media-worthy crime. (I'm not encouraging you to break the law here, but please remember what this did for Cynthia Payne, Streatham brothel-keeper. She was even immortalised in two films about her life, *Personal Services* and *Wish You Were Here*.)

Some areas offer far more scope for high visibility than others – entertainment, politics and sport are all good bets. With the exception of Michael Heseltine (who studied to be one then changed direction into politics) it's quite difficult to think, for instance, of a celebrity accountant. . . .

High-visibility celebrity is often short-lived, so you can understand people wanting to cash in on it. You don't have to become a celebrity to increase your visibility; what you are doing is making more people aware of who you are and what you do. These people

may be confined to a professional sector or your local community.
Increasing your visibility can help you:

- Become more prominent in your profession.

- Get publicity and money for a business, organisation, association
  or cause.

Some people, like Anita Roddick of the Body Shop, successfully use
their visibility to do all of these things.

THE DOWN-SIDE OF VISIBILITY

If you become highly visible, more people will want to be associated
with you. If you have always been accessible, constraints on your
time may mean that you have to make yourself less so. And if the
number of people who admire you increases, so will the number of
detractors: the more publicity you attract, the more some people
will want to criticise you. In 'going public' you also become more
vulnerable. The photographer David Bailey, according to some of
the press a 'difficult' interviewee, recently voiced the opinion that if
you own up and talk about your achievements to journalists you get
described as 'big-headed'; on the other hand, if you underplay them
you get described as 'pretentiously modest'.

Some highly visible people start to believe their own publicity.
Sudden exposure throws them off balance and makes them
insecure, so they start to behave in a self-important way. Their own
sense of identity gets distorted and they start to believe that who the
media say they are is true. Being over-susceptible to the attention of
others, they can lose their way.

The wider your association with different people and agendas,
the more discriminating you need to be about your values and
motivation. And increased visibility can mean you suffer reduced
credibility, especially among your peers. An expert is asked by a
furniture company to lead a survey researching people's sleeping
habits. The company has just launched a new type of bed. The
results of the survey attract publicity. They show that a large number of people have problems sleeping. The expert is asked to go on a
television chat show, involving travel to another part of the
country. She would prefer to spend her weekend at home. The

furniture company, however, offers her an irresistible sum of money to appear. She is to mention the survey and the company's name. She is on air for about a minute and loses no sleep over her decision . . . The bulk of the viewing audience were probably not even aware that she had plugged the company, let alone that she was being paid handsomely for it. Presumably fellow 'experts' would not view the appearance and subtle advertising with similar innocence.

If you become well-known outside the confines of your own field, you may find that your 'celebrity status' affects and reduces your 'expert status' among close peers. Some of this must be down to jealousy and resentment: when you get exposure outside your immediate circle, your influence is spreading. There is also a sense that if you show an ability to communicate through and use the media, and spend time and energy doing so, you must be spending less time on your 'expert' activity – that you're becoming more of a 'generalist' than a 'specialist'. Your high visibility damages your eligibility for the membership of an exclusive club. Some people will say that you've 'sold out' and be envious that you've had the opportunity to do so.

The demands of increasing your visibility and gaining personal power may be tiring and time-consuming. For instance, if you get on the committee of a professional association you might find that the time available for your leisure activities and family decreases. If you're working hard promoting a business or charity, you might find that your phone is constantly ringing and at all hours. People will have expectations of you, and if you're speaking in public several times a month, however much you enjoy it you may start to get exhausted.

Flattered by the attention and wanting to be generous, you may find it difficult to say no to people who ask you for advice and support. You might find that you have to start to ration your time and attention very carefully. You may gain contacts but lose friends. These drawbacks considered, the rewards of visibility are still, in many people's minds, worth it.

USING YOUR VISIBILITY

There are pictures of the SDP conference in every national newspaper. Why? John Cleese is in the photos, on the conference

119

platform endorsing the policies of the SDP. His attendance and visibility get the party badly needed exposure.

Once a person gets well known, he or she will be in demand, and can use that demand to champion various interests and causes. John Cleese, for instance, having gained fame in *Monty Python's Flying Circus*, then went on to make *Fawlty Towers*, to establish the highly successful Video Arts Training Film company, to write about and make public his interest in psychotherapy and to make party political broadcasts for the SDP. He has gone on to ally himself with royalty and the Green cause, heavily publicising a film starring himself and Prince Charles, which was aimed at increasing 'green' awareness in business. Dolly Parton, Goldie Hawn, Glenda Jackson and Jane Fonda have all successfully moved from straight performing roles into business or politics. Sir John Harvey Jones, having risen to become chairman of ICI, went on to write a book and then to present a television series in which he played 'company doctor' to ailing businesses.

These 'Renaissance people' show how, once you have gained recognition and credibility, it is easier to spread your influence and get exposure for your other interests. You can diversify and create and take opportunities. You can have far more choice and control over what you do. Other people, business and causes are keen to be associated with you because of your reputation. Your personal influence spreads and so too does your range of options.

With increased visibility you can make more money, though the two do not necessarily go hand-in-hand. You need business sense or advisers to capitalise on your exposure. You have to have the 'right image', too; female sportswomen are less likely to be offered product endorsement deals if there is any suspicion that they could be gay, for instance. Martina Navratilova was, of course, an exception, her status and celebrity being so high that this condition was waived.

People very often associate exposure and publicity with endorsement of worth. This is irrational, but many of us still do it. If you're written about in your company magazine, you will assume a certain status with the readers in that you are seen as sufficiently significant to warrant a mention. If there's an article in a trade paper on your company, the same assumption may be made. When the charity you work for gets a five-minute mention on your local television news programme, many of the viewers will assume unconsciously that it warrants this airtime because of the good work being done. Reputation spreads, and when people know who you are and what you do you can ask for more money, gain clients and customers and raise more from donations.

From your own point of view, visibility can be enormously gratifying. Other people are giving you and your achievements recognition. Your profession, peer group, local community or the public are confirming that you matter. You have some prominence and influence, and this can reinforce and increase your sense of personal power.

YOUR STRATEGY

Your strategy for increasing your own visibility, or that of a business, organisation or cause, will depend on your specific objective. In every instance, though, there are five stages that are useful:

- Assessing current position and resources – asking yourself 'where am I and what have I/we got?'

- Researching your 'market' – asking 'What/who else is on offer?' and 'Who will buy this?'

- Developing your 'product' – asking 'what do I/we need to do to improve?'

- Publicising your 'product' – asking 'Where and how can I/we do this?'

- Getting commitment and maintaining visibility – 'How do I/we capitalise on exposure and keep visible?'

PROMOTING YOURSELF

Assessing Your Position and Resources

In the same way that marketing and advertising people will regard a product or a service as a person, ascribing to it qualities such as 'friendly', 'concerned' or 'resilient' to help them think creatively, it can be a useful exercise to think objectively about yourself as a product or service. If you were a marketing person how would you sell yourself? Have you been on the same shelves too long? Is your packaging out-of-date? Are you under-priced? Do you have a 'unique selling proposition?' (marketing jargon for 'What makes you different from everyone else?'). On courses in interview skills training, this exercise proves useful in going some way to overcoming the British propensity towards modesty.

Look at your history, your current position and where you want to be next. Set yourself one or several achievable objectives; promotion in a year's time, for instance, or a move to another business within six months. Be flexible about your objectives. Some people constantly set themselves unrealistic objectives that they constantly fail to achieve and use this as a justification for self-recrimination. Flexibility can be a useful approach. Your objectives, after all, serve to give you a clear sense of direction. If you follow them in a blinkered fashion, you may miss out on opportunities. So set them, and be prepared to change them when appropriate.

Your most useful resources are:

- *People*
  Whom do you know who can help you get promotion, change jobs, speak at conferences? Have you got contacts from the past who are now in a position to help you? Is it worth seeking advice from a career counsellor? Is there someone influential who can act as your backer or champion? (People often find it flattering to be asked to do this; it's an acknowledgement of their power.)

- *Time*
  When do you and your contacts have time to get together to talk? Is it worth giving up your aerobics classes or golf games for a while so that you can concentrate on self-promotion? Can you give up an evening a week or some time at the weekends?

- *Money*
  Are you financially in a position where you could stop working for a while in order to concentrate on changing direction? Can you afford to go on training courses/do a part-time MBA/buy some new clothes?

- *Your skills and interests*
  Evaluate what you are good at, what you like doing and how you can capitalise on this. If you write well, can you call up a trade paper or magazine and offer to write an article? If you talk well, can you make an internal presentation on something of interest to other departments? Or give a talk about what you do to a

professional organisation? Are you involved in a hobby that you could make into a career? If you like dealing with people, can you move from a technical role into personnel? The more fulfilled you are in using your skills and interests, the greater the likelihood of achieving visibility.

Researching Your 'Market'

Marketing is all about the bringing together of what's on offer and what the market needs, expects and demands. When it is yourself that's on offer, you need to position and mould yourself so that you meet market requirements. Information power is everything here. If you don't know already, find out where the best jobs are in your business, who's doing them and how they got there. Analyse the qualities that they are renowned and prized for. You can use the top people as role models, remembering that you are unique and that conditions change. Sometimes top people in an organisation are out-of-date with the current climate and hold their positions merely by virtue of the fact that they've been there a long time.

Britain is a comparatively small country, which makes it easy to gather a great deal of information about what is going on in your field. Avid information gathering from newspapers about latest developments and trends can prove invaluable. Subscribe to trade papers and find out what conferences and exhibitions are coming up and whether they are worth attending.

Your market is anyone who employs and can help people with your talent and skills. Be aware of your employers' competitors and their relative status. One of the most useful means of increasing visibility is through association: as a representative of a company with an excellent record of customer care, you're more likely to be asked to speak at a conference on this subject than if you work for a company with a moderately good record. If it looks as though your company is going through a period of change and uncertainty, with its reputation falling and your potential not fully realised, you may want to look around for better opportunities. Are you in the best marketplace for your abilities?

Find out about formal and informal networks and join them. In this way you can extend your visibility outside your immediate working environment. Through meeting people in the same field, and establishing your presence at events, you can build contacts.

Starting a network yourself where one is needed is a good method of gaining visibility.

Compare who you are, and how you represent yourself and your abilities, against a background of market trends: demographic, economic, technological, political, social and cultural influences. For instance:

- Are you living and working in the best place to get noticed?
- Are economic factors affecting the demand for your services?
- Do you need to acquire technical skills to keep up with advances?
- Will a change in government or legislation help you become more prominent?
- Does the way you represent yourself reflect the trends and aspirations of current society and culture? (Note, for example, how often high-visibility people are currently mentioning family and 'green' values in their public utterances.)

Developing Your 'Product'

When you are the 'product' you can do a great deal to develop 'market appeal'. You may not want to go as far as Allen Konigsberg, Bette Joan Berske and Marion Morrison, who respectively became Woody Allen, Lauren Bacall and John Wayne, but the way that you represent yourself, the distinctive 'role' you play, can increase your visibility.

Your 'product' must be able to do what you claim it can. Check how you regard your skills, contrasted with the skills your role models have, and if necessary build on your existing ability. Be tactical about this and use common sense. For instance, if your company is about to be German-owned, then learning the language would be a shrewd move. The importance of formal skills and qualifications can be over-estimated; it's all too easy to think: 'If I get enough letters after my name, I should be OK.' Alan Sugar, the founder of Amstrad (and the Chairman of Tottenham Hotspur), and John Major are good examples of high-visibility people with few formal qualifications. Getting more and more qualifications is no substitute for push and determination. Some people avoid real life by remaining 'perpetual students'.

Research training courses and refine your presentation and communication skills. These days there are courses available to meet most needs – from Influencing Skills via Telephone Techniques to Dealing with Difficult People. Check that your appearance and manner are working to your advantage – if not, then study the subject of impression management (see Chapter Seven) or seek professional advice. Bear in mind how you described yourself as a product, and that descriptions like 'strong', 'reliable' and 'outgoing' are conveyed as much through how you look, dress and sound as by what you say.

Use your best channels for communication. Julie Burchill, high-profile, much-publicised journalist, apparently has a weak, high-pitched voice, so other journalists tell us. (Few of us have heard it.) Unlike many other celebrity journalists who welcome radio and television exposure, she is conspicuous by her absence. But she maintains a high profile through diversifying in her writing; along with print journalism she writes plays and sexbuster novels (for which she gets a lot of newspaper coverage). And the image of her that we get from her vituperative prose is not jeopardised by our hearing her speak.

Communicating your aims and achievements to people effectively is also important. Your boss should know that you want promotion, unless he or she is likely to block it. Let people know that you want to write articles and make presentations. So what if they think you're pushy, and so what if they choose not to take you up on your offer? They are not rejecting you personally – they are rejecting a course of action you wish to take. They may even regret this decision.

If you've been brought up not to be pushy, you may find approaching people like newspaper editors difficult. Remember that one of the easiest ways to do this, if you fear rejection, is to ask people for advice. So you could ring an editor and ask them to advise you whether they would be interested in an article along the lines that you suggest. If they say no, you can ask them for suggestions as to where you might be able to place it. You could write to the events organiser at your professional association, and ask for advice as to whether your talk might be appropriate for an evening meeting. If not, they may have suggestions as to who else might be interested. Include mention of your achievements and areas of specialisation. Above all, remember your unique selling proposition – what is it that makes you distinctive, unusual and different?

When you approach people, remember that *you* are helping *them*. We're talking about equal levels of status here, and if the person you approach behaves in a dismissive manner it is they who have the problem. Don't waste your time pursuing them. Feature editors, radio and television producers and organisers of associations and networks are always on the look-out for people with new ideas and original material. The one you have this time may not be appropriate – you could, however, be a valuable source of material in the future.

Publicising Your 'Product'

Professional publicists take care that celebrities are exposed through the right channels. When the Labour party in Britain wanted to appeal to the youth market they used Billy Bragg, a popular protest singer, as a 'front man' and Neil Kinnock appeared in a pop video. It's up to you whether you think a pop video is a suitable vehicle for a potential Prime Minister; certainly the stunt must have reinforced the viewpoint held by some that Mr Kinnock had insufficient *gravitas*. And when the young royals appeared horsing around in the television show *It's a Knockout* the view was widely expressed that it was inappropriate exposure for a family that is expected to represent dignity and ceremony.

When the product is yourself, you need to place yourself so that you get the right type of exposure to the right sort of people. You need to be discriminating and focused and to keep asking yourself, 'Is this helping me go in my chosen direction?' Publicity for the sake of publicity may result in your getting over-exposed and losing credibility.

At the risk of appearing fussy, state and check how you want to be 'billed' before you speak, or at the end of an article. Many the public speaker who has had to work hard to build credibility after a bumbling, inaccurate introduction by a nervous chairperson. Your reputation is significant for your visibility, and for many of us it's more comfortably established by a third party. Whenever possible, write down how you would like to be introduced or credited. This advice comes from someone who was once introduced, prior to a ninety-minute address to an audience of a hundred, as resembling a 'manic garden gnome'.

Whenever you write or speak to groups, bear in mind what marketing people call 'sector expectations'. How does your audience expect you to represent yourself, and what specific concerns and aspirations can you appeal to? Sometimes it can be effective to undermine these expectations and in doing so attract more attention and prominence. La Ciccolina, the Italian porn star, undermines people's expectations of a member of parliament. In marked contrast, Anita Roddick in her casual clothes going on backpacking trips undermined stereotypical expectations of the image of the 1980s businesswoman.

Undermining expectations can be risky – you need to be sure of the values of the people to whom you are appealing and of their concerns at that time – otherwise you may cause offence. However, you are more likely to get visibility by being controversial than by sitting on the fence – having ensured, of course, that your arguments are backed up by valid reasoning. Because so few people come out and express opinions voluntarily, those who do often gain admiration and respect. One of the best examples of undermining expectations occurs when a politician gives a direct reply to a question in a television or radio interview. It's such an unusual occurrence, and so contrary to what we are used to, that many of us sit up and take notice – and then his or her credibility soars.

Maintaining Visibility

Once you have gained some visibility, made your presentations, spoken at a conference, written an article or presented a paper, you need to maintain and build on this exposure. Where else can you deliver a similar message, and can you cross over from one medium to another? You might have written an article for a local newspaper, for instance, on developing your own small business. Could you adapt this for the Small Business Association's magazine, or give a talk based on it to your local Chamber of Commerce? Send a copy of the article to potentially interested parties.

Say you're giving a talk to local women returning to work. Can you give this to formalised networks of women returners, or at conferences concerned with this issue, or to national associations and employers? Could you change your talk into an article and get it published? Your motto could be 'Ever vigilant for opportunities'.

Maintaining visibility is all to do with maintaining contacts. When you get an opportunity to promote yourself thank the people who gave it to you, preferably in writing, which has more sense of permanence than a phone call. If your expertise is sufficiently established, you may become an 'expert source' in the future and your opinions may be quoted in articles and interviews. Keep channels of communication open, and keep people informed on what you are up to. You and your contacts can be of mutual benefit to one another.

Like politicians, be seen everywhere. Unless you're on the campaign trail, you don't need to stoop to endless kissing of babies to provide photo opportunities. But if you've recently had some sort of exposure through print, the media or addressing large audiences, reinforce your high profile by attending meetings, conferences and exhibitions where you can renew acquaintances.

A few years ago, Sir James Goldsmith, the international financier, announced his intention of devoting his energies to the preservation of rainforests. More recently, he announced the formation of a 'referendum party' – a political party dedicated to questioning the Maastricht Treaty. He reinvents his image in accordance with what he considers to be appropriate to the time we live in. To maintain and increase visibility, it's important to be in tune with the time. And this can be very immediate. For example, if a news story breaks that the government are passing legislation to improve the lot of working mothers, and you have something as a reputation for writing about and talking to women returners, you could ring round features editors and TV and radio researchers and let them know that you are available for comment. Even if they don't use you this time, your name can be added to their 'useful contacts' lists.

Visibility gives you an opportunity to diversify, and that very diversification can widen your 'sector' appeal. High-visibility people may reinvent themselves and change role according to the prevailing climate; Jane Fonda, for instance, has gone from Barbarella to Hanoi Jane, to fitness queen, to politician and then to media mogul's consort. The key to survival in maintaining visibility is, as in many activities, adaptability.

When you promote yourself you are also, as I have mentioned earlier, able to promote your business, association or concerns. You are a highly visible ambassador or representative for them. Here are some further pointers on how to achieve results in this field.

PROMOTING YOUR BUSINESS OR ORGANISATION

Assessing Current Resources

The organisation of people, time, money and skills is again import-ant. If you're starting up or already running something you'll need to work out how you are going to use your time, how much money you need for marketing and publicity, what people can help you and the skills that you need to get from others. You may need to use the services of solicitors and accountants, and therefore to budget for these. Provided that you are not in direct competition, other people in established businesses and organisations may be prepared to give you some time and advice.

In seeking to increase the visibility of your business or organisa-tion your goal must be to make it expand. You therefore need to set goals for your expansion, and to make them realistic and achiev-able. Can you meet demand if it dramatically increases? Too rapid an expansion can be dangerous, particularly in an unpredictable economic climate.

You'll need to decide on the emphasis for promotion, and that will depend on your goals. You may decide, for instance, to become highly visible yourself in order to get publicity (like Victor Kiam with Remington, Bernard Matthews with his turkeys or Sheila McKechnie, when she worked at Shelter). If your long-term plans are to sell your business in several years, then you may have made yourself indispensable and this could be a drawback. Alternatively, your long-term plans may be to sell your business with you still retaining a consultancy and/or publicity function, in the way that John Cleese has done with Video Arts. You may want to get a well-known patron for your organisation who can publicise it and who benefits from the association in the way, for instance, that Glenda Jackson is the patron of a drama school.

Rather than concentrating on the people involved, you may decide that you want to emphasise the function, services or prod-ucts that you want to promote. You can't keep promotion 'people-free', but the content of your promotional material can focus on what the business does rather than who does it. Indeed, if the head of a successful business strictly rations their media exposure they can increase their value. Alan Sugar of Amstrad, for instance, rarely gives interviews and press conferences. When he does give one, rarity value ensures that the coverage is extensive.

There may be schemes available to help you with promotion. A few years ago, the Post Office, for instance, offered a 'start-up' scheme to new businesses: if you mailed a thousand leaflets or brochures, then, subject to the Post Office checking that you were not sending anything seditious, you got the mailing free. It is worth contacting your local TEC and the Department of Trade and Industry to find out whether there are any schemes operating for which you may be eligible.

Researching Your Market

Find out how similar businesses and organisations promote themselves. Send off for all their publicity material, check if and where they advertise, and who their clients are. You don't have to do things the same way, though. Anita Roddick, for example, unlike the rest of the retail sector, chooses not to advertise the Body Shop. She relies on other methods of publicity – mainly word of mouth, direct mail, and extensive editorial achieved through excellent public relations with customers and the media.

Be as specific as you can about whom you are trying to reach. Though it can be tempting to try and get visibility on a wide scale, 'narrowcasting' (as contrasted with broadcasting) is often a more effective long-term tactic. When you 'narrowcast' you start to promote to a small, clearly defined group of people who will provide you with a small but committed market – a solid base of custom. When you 'narrowcast' you appeal to your market's sense of exclusivity, of being in a select group who are in the know. This appeal to exclusive status may be reflected in your prices. Imagine that you are promoting a business providing a domestic service, say ironing or gardening. It makes sense initially to target a small group of people above a certain level of income who live in a certain area, and to publicise your business heavily in this sector. When you've built up sufficient predictable repeat custom here, you may want to make your business visible elsewhere. Of course, for this to work you have to have sufficient takers in your targeted sector. For the impatient this can seem a slow and plodding approach to promotion; the solid base it creates, however, can ensure long-term survival.

When marketing companies are testing a new image or product

they often use market feasibility groups to gauge response. A small sample group of perhaps six or seven people representing the projected market will be asked for their reaction, which will be filmed for analysis. When you're promoting a new business or organisation you may want to do your own informal feasibility study. Think of people you know who are potential customers and ask them what they think of your ideas. Find out what newspapers, magazines and television programmes they watch, so that you can start to draw up a more detailed picture of a typical customer.

Advertising and marketing people use all sorts of sophisticated systems for defining and classifying customer groups. Here are some rudimentary questions that you will find it helpful to answer before working out where and how to seek publicity:

- How can I define my market in terms of age, gender, profession, income, family status, where they live, what their interests are, what they read, what they listen to on radio and look at on television?

- How can I define my market in terms of their values and beliefs? What instincts am I appealing to (for instance aggression, competitiveness, self-improvement, nurture, vanity, sex, fear)? How does what I am selling identify with people's needs (for physiological, security, social, self-esteem and self-realisation needs – see Chapter Four)?

- What have I got in common with my market, and how can I indicate that we have shared interests and understanding? How can I show that my business is different from the competition?

- And once again – what's in it for them?

Publicising Your 'Product'

When you are setting up a business or organisation, one of the best ways of letting people know that you are doing so is through the 'who's moved where' slot of a specialist newspaper or magazine. Angling your publicity so that it emphasises the new, the innovative and a 'first' will always help you make news.

If you've got something to give away that looks good, so much the better. This can just be a brochure explaining what your company or organisation does. If it looks aesthetically pleasing, with colours, typography, design and content accurately representing the appropriate image, then people are more likely to hang on to it. This is important if you are attending exhibitions and speaking at conferences. It's an upmarket approach to the 'FREE GIFT!!!!' idea.

The boundaries between a small business and an organisation can be faint. Organisations are set up to provide networks and often to provide a meeting place for business-to-business trading. At a meeting you make a contact who proves useful to you, and later on you are able to use their services yourself. Some organisations mail on behalf of members for a fee. If you start or join an organisation connected with your professional role and you become its chairperson, inevitably your professional status will rise as you are publicised.

You may even decide to start a newsletter yourself, aimed at increasing membership, giving members information and publicising your own activities and those of other members. The grey area of the boundaries between organisations and businesses is often exploited: people may set up something called an 'institute' or 'association' purely as a money-making exercise, when to many of us those descriptions have misleading connotations of 'learning' and 'advancement'. Mr P., for instance, has a business that trains the staff of companies and organisations in how to represent themselves well and sell at exhibitions. Mr P. starts up an association for exhibitors with a newsletter which he distributes at exhibitions. Is it any surprise that the newsletter is full of what Mr P. has on offer? The packaging and approach are highly deceptive.

Besides the obvious channels like press, television and radio, exhibition and conference coverage, you may want to publicise your business or organisation through social or educational events. You may decide to hold a launch party at which the press and potential customers are wined, dined, informed and entertained. If you can get celebrities associated with what you do, so much the better. When a royal is seen to be at your restaurant, buying your deodorant, using your exercise plan or eating your health food, you've hit the bigtime.

Seminars and 'sampling events' can also provide a good shop window. Fashion shows, food and drink tasting opportunities and training courses are all 'tasters' to increase your visibility.

Maintaining Visibility

When your business or organisation is established, you need to find ways of keeping it visible. When the Body Shop expanded, franchisees were encouraged to establish and maintain excellent relations with local journalists, so that public relations was intensified in a wider geographical area. Members of an organisation may be able to do the same thing – to create local interest to increase the profile (and, of course, to get themselves some personal publicity as well).

It's likely that you'll have more money available and you may need to use some of this for publicity. John Fenton, a sales-training guru who already enjoyed an excellent reputation, wanted to increase his visibility dramatically. So he hired the Albert Hall to hold a conference. This was a 'loss leader' for him at the time, and cost him a lot of money. A few years later, though, he was able to sell his company for several million pounds.

Some businesses and organisations may find advertising useful, but for many people public relations are a lot more effective (it's estimated that editorial brings in ten times as much business as advertising). You may decide that you can afford and need to use the services of a professional public relations company (see p. 140).

Once you've got some visibility, it may be useful to think of ways of diversifying to maintain it. What can you introduce that is new and that will get publicity? Like Anita Roddick, Paula Yates, John Harvey Jones, John Cleese and many others, could you write a book about your views? A publisher is likely to be receptive to the idea if he or she knows that you are high-profile in your marketplace, already well known to your customers and clients, which will guarantee a certain number of sales. If you don't have the time or inclination to write about what you do, then the publisher will provide you with a 'ghost' writer. Either way, your book itself may not make much money – but it will maintain your visibility.

New products and services that are newsworthy will help you maintain visibility. Successful hairdressers start to market products bearing their names, to write books about hair, to appear on television. Can what you do be effectively represented on cassette and/or video?

PROMOTING A CAUSE

Again, much of the above advice is relevant. Some further considerations include:

Assessing Your Resources

When you're championing a cause, people and money are your most important resources. And when people are giving their time and skills for no material return, they need a lot of recognition and acknowledgement. Bob Geldof is the great example of someone who used his own celebrity and celebrity contacts to champion a cause. Remember that celebrities are keen to be associated with charities to maintain their own visibility and to temper an image of being too self-serving. To temper an image of being too cynical, I must suggest that some of them genuinely care. . . . When you are using the help of a celebrity, though, it's worth ensuring that your cause is benefiting as much as, if not more than, they are.

Your goals may include a certain sum of money, opening a charity shop, or getting a certain number of patrons on your side.

Researching Your Market

Your market is whom to approach for money and support. If you're fighting the building of a new by-pass research previous similar protests, get in touch with the people involved and use the methods that proved successful. People running other charities can be approached for advice.

Your trump card is that you are asking people to help others, and that businesses and organisations like to be seen to be caring. Charity 'telethons' make most of their money on this basis.

Market forces need to be considered, especially cultural and social values. Certain 'good causes' become fashionable according to trends. In the present climate Aids and 'green' causes are the darlings of the socially prominent. Take every opportunity to link your cause to news items.

Publicising Your Cause

Find out which local and national print and broadcast journalists champion causes, and keep them informed on what you are doing. Jill Morrell, campaigning on behalf of John McCarthy and the other hostages in Beirut, was well placed to do so in that she works in the media. Even so, she extended her campaign to include organising concerts on John's behalf and getting an advertising agency to produce a provocative film and poster as publicity.

Nowadays fund-raising for charities is extremely inventive. The 'social' aspects of an appeal are very important: people like to come together for a theatrical performance, food and drink or fashion show and feel that they are 'doing good'. If the CD/celebrity cookbook/Christmas cards are attractively packaged, so much the better; we can please ourselves while feeling that we are also helping others. You'll always do better if you can offer people a good time for their money.

Undermining expectations and using shock tactics work well in dispelling myths about do-gooders. David Bailey's film for Lynx, in which models paraded on the catwalk in furs and the audience and floor became spattered with blood; Bob Geldof railing and swearing at us to give money to Live Aid; and the RSPCA's poster showing a great heap of dead dogs, are all examples of this.

LOSING VISIBILITY

Publicity and exposure come in waves, and celebrity is always threatened by the fickle nature of the public. Whatever field you become prominent in, as you get older you may find your motivation and ability dwindling. Your priorities may change. As 'insurance' on maintaining visibility, think about:

- Keeping up with changing trends.

- Broadening 'sector' appeal; that is, widening your target audience.

- Diversifying into other areas

- Guarding against over-exposure, and believing your own publicity.

- Avoiding scandal – though that doesn't seem to have jinxed the careers of Jeffrey Archer or Cecil Parkinson. Perhaps that should read 'encourage scandal. . .'?

APPROACHING THE PRESS

Whatever your purpose in increasing your visibility, you will find it useful to consider the following:

- It's worth targeting several types of newspapers and magazines – what you have to say may fit into several different categories. Consider local press, specialist and trade publications, general magazines, national newspapers and their magazine sections, Saturday newspaper magazines, Sunday papers and their supplements. Categories you may want to consider include:

News	Calendars of forthcoming
Business	events
People profiles	'What's new' sections
Society page	Photo opportunities
Women's page	Education
Lifestyle page	Media
Consumer items	Science and technology
Human interest –	Fashion
people, children and	Gossip
animals	Travel

- Your coverage is far more likely to be read if it's accompanied by a photograph. When you send press releases it may be worth getting some photographs taken (10 × 8 ins) in black and white, especially if you or somebody else involved is photogenic. The simpler and more striking the photograph the better. The larger newspapers will often supply their own photographers, but trade and specialist press may be glad to use what you send them.

  Get a photo taken vertically rather than horizontally. Then if they crop it it is guaranteed to take up at least one column. When you're publicising a company or organisation, get your logo in the background if you can. And for some newspapers, if you can get a baby or an animal into the photograph – well, so much the better. . . . Finally, the back of your photograph should have the names and positions of the people shown clearly marked.

- Some stories and themes constantly appear in the press, and you will find it useful to angle your approaches accordingly. These include:

The first ever	Tragedy
The last ever	Dramatic change in
Local boy or girl makes good	fortune
Threats to security	Success and failure
Conflict and rivalry	Eccentricity
Conspicuous consumption	Failure to meet standards
Disadvantaged person makes	Innovation
good	Behaviour and lifestyle
Tips on self-improvement	analysis
Injustice	Strong principles
Outrageous behaviour	Sensational crime
The environment	Results of a survey

Press Releases

Public relations companies use a Who, What, When, Where, Why, How formula for deciding what to put into press releases. If you can tie your angle into current news and trends, so much the better. The more that journalists can see that they can 'lift' from the release, the more likely they are to use it, so study current press preoccupations and angle accordingly.

Keep your release short, and type it using double spacing. Use direct facts, and cite opinions in the form of quotations. Avoid flowery language and adjectives. Get a strong, punchy headline and indicate where the release ends. Put the date clearly at the top of the page and then either 'FOR IMMEDIATE RELEASE' or 'FOR RELEASE AFTER [DATE].' If journalists want further information, they should be able clearly to see a name and daytime and evening telephone numbers. If you're sending the same release to several people on the same publication, indicate that this has been done.

When you've got a good contact in a journalist, you may want to send them an 'exclusive' release. Call them to check whether they want to use it, and if they don't you can circulate the information.

Maintain up-to-date records of your press contacts so that they are kept in touch with your activities. If a journalist writes a feature on you, be prepared for unpredictability in its publication. It may be planned for a day following a disaster or outbreak of war – in which case you will have to wait for your exposure.

Use your press clippings to keep customers and clients informed and interested, and if the coverage is local it may be worth sending to the nationals. Remember that the knock-on effect of newspaper exposure can be considerable, so be prepared for approaches from radio and television companies, whose researchers are constantly combing the newspapers for stories. Your fifteen minutes may have arrived.

RADIO AND TELEVISION VISIBILITY

Where appropriate, send your press releases to radio and television programmes. If you're an 'expert' of some description and can be interviewed, get your name and contact number on the resource list, their information file. Send the relevant people your press clippings and CV, and if you want to call them your best chance of getting through is just after the programme has been on air. Local radio and television appearances can be very good training for the wider audience of national networks.

When radio and television companies contact you, make sure that you understand what the item is about, how long it will run and what role you've been cast in. Check out who else is appearing and whether your appearance (on television especially) is definitely confirmed. This advice comes from someone who was hauled off to a TV station very early in the morning only to be told, when she got there, that she was just a 'stand-in'. At least she got a fee. . . .

Researchers and editors may 'interview' you over the phone to check your suitability and to prepare content. If they take you by surprise, ask if you can return their call in a few minutes and meanwhile sort out what you want to say. Bear in mind the specific audience and their interests. If you're commenting on business, for example, a mid-morning radio or television programme is going to have a very different audience with different concerns from a business news programme which goes on air at 7 p.m.

As to your actual performance, the following suggestions may be useful:

• Prepare as much as you can beforehand. Don't expect the interviewer to use what the researcher may have laboriously prepared. Politicians are transparently trained to make three points concerning their particular agenda. Avoid 'learning your lines' but get your ideas together, work out how you can express them succinctly, and have facts and statistics at your fingertips when appropriate to back them up.

- It's useful to talk to the interviewer beforehand if possible. They won't inevitably be 'out to get you' – it depends on the programme. Here are some familiar 'dodges' to difficult questions frequently used by our politicians: 'That's an interesting question and what I'd like to say is. . . .' (Note the careful use of language here. If the speaker used 'but what I'd like to say is . . .' we'd all be more aware of what was going on); 'I think the real issue/priority here. . . .'; 'Now I think that what you're really asking is. . . .'

  Interviewers dislike interviewees who are very evasive. It's insulting to their status as 'investigative journalists' and to our status as viewers. They patronise us in that they seem to think they can pull the wool over our eyes. When challenged, it's better to take some responsibility, answer the question, even accept some culpability and then go on to talk about positives.

- However 'under attack' you feel, maintain a good-humoured, positive attitude and keep your behaviour under control. Attacking the interviewer back is rarely successful. Try and relax as much as you can beforehand – warm up your voice and face, and smile as you're introduced. Keep your body language still and open. There is evidence that viewers make up their minds about people appearing on television in the first fifteen seconds of airtime.

- In discussion programmes get in early and don't shy away from interrupting. Listen to what the other participants have to say and pick up on that, rather than storming through with your own agenda. Treat other people with respect, even if their views are very different from your own. 'Bully tactics' are low on appeal. Use short sentences, rather than long, convoluted ramblings, and make your points succinctly.

- The airwaves offer a great opportunity for plugging whatever it is you are selling. However, programmers dislike overt sales pitches and plugs. When someone repeatedly drops in the name of their 'product' there is little difference between programming and adverts – apart from the fact that the latter may be more entertaining. The best way to plug something you are associated with is to check that the interviewer or presenter is briefed about it and then ask them to mention it. They'll be very familiar with this request.

USING PROFESSIONAL PR COMPANIES

In the past two decades, the public relations industry has grown considerably. PR men like Peter Mandleson MP and Sir Tim Bell have become celebrities themselves, and fill up column inches with their own profiles.

PR companies exist to communicate information between companies, individuals and their clients, customers and audiences. The range of activities they get involved in could include managing media coverage, writing press releases, staging press conferences, organising speaking events and tours, and training and image consultancy.

A lot of highly visible people are their own best PR representatives. For many others, professional public relations advice is a sound investment:

- When you're embarking on a publicity campaign for the first time, and you're unsure how to proceed.

- When your business or cause grows to such a size that you don't have time to maintain your own public relations.

- If you've a one-off special project coming up, for which you want extensive coverage.

- Finally, if disaster strikes and your image, or that of your business or cause, is damaged, skilled public relations may help to put it right. Public relations people are experts in creating and placing 'strategic' stories in the press. So when Fergie seems to have hit an all-time low in popularity, we suddenly find a spate of pictures and stories regarding the 'good works' that she's involved in. That's public relations in action.

As the head of a small company or organisation, you may find a public relations company of similar size best suited to your needs.

Check that they don't have too many clients, and that they special-
ise in your area. Be sure that you can have clear, open communication with them because you want their interpretation of your
strengths to be the same as yours – they're telling your story. Make
sure that you understand exactly what's on offer for your money.
And finally, remember that they may guarantee to get you coverage,
but in the instance of something like a restaurant review they may
not be able to guarantee the *quality* of that coverage. Along with
many others, you might decide that it's better to be talked about
badly than. . .

THE LAST RESORT

Still seeking visibility? For the ever-hungry self-publicist, here are
some final 'do or die' ideas:

- Get people to page you and your company repeatedly at airports,
  preferably densely busy ones like Heathrow.

- Keep phoning in on radio call-in shows – the same people do it
  all the time.

- Maintain a steady stream of letters to a cross-section of
  newspapers and magazines.

- Get on Channel 4 – in the video box or on *Right to Reply* – or,
  depending on your orientation, *Blind Date* or *Mastermind*.

- Keep doing the pools.

- Start your own political party, preferably one with a long, silly
  name.

- Invent a diet.

chapter six

POWERFUL PEOPLE

There is always room at the top.
Daniel Webster, US statesman

This chapter will look at the qualities people need to succeed and get recognition, how to cope with people who are pre-occupied with their own power, and how to handle the responsibilities that power can bring. It contains more tactical advice, as well as suggestions on how to use some of the previously mentioned techniques in specific situations.

CHARACTERISTICS OF SUCCESS

We like to think that there's some secret to success, and that were we to possess it then we would achieve our goals. Despite the Victor Kiams and the Donald Trumps of this world earning a few bucks more out of revealing their 'secrets' in books, there really is no set formula. For example, we could describe a lot of successful people as 'confident'; but then there are prominent artists, writers and academics – people who spend a great deal of time in solitary, contemplative activity – who are extremely shy and reclusive. It's even likely that this disposition has contributed to their success; less keen to go out and mingle as children and/or adults, they have spent more time in solitude pursuing their goals. Some actors and entertainers are shy; one of the attractions of their chosen profession, perhaps, being the security of disguise. Mike Yarwood, the impersonator, has had a long and much-publicised battle with crippling shyness.

People use different methods for getting and maintaining power. Some will place emphasis on delegation and education so that their influence spreads and continues, while others will use their positional power and the authority contained within it to further their cause. Yet others will actively use the media so that their recognition and expert status spreads.

What is certain is that when powerful people start to believe that:

- they are invulnerable;

- their own opinion is the only one worth listening to;

- their power as represented by the media is accurate;

- they should do things as they've always done them before, regardless of circumstances . . .

then they put their power in jeopardy. Like leaders, people often get power because the time and situation are right for what they have to offer. Circumstances and climates change, and inflexibility, which was once a virtue, can become a drawback.

Here's a quote from Yvette Newbold (who was company secretary of Hanson Industrial Conglomerate until 1995, and is now chief executive of Proned), one of the few women at the very top of corporate Britain:

> I have always tried to look for opportunities. I don't so much plan my career as say to myself, 'Right, that sounds interesting and challenging, I'll give it a go.' I am highly energetic and goal-oriented. I never planned in detail. I just thought, 'Well, hell I'd like to be a director.'
>
> If I have any advice it is do not give up. Don't be faint-hearted when things seem a bit slow or boring. I feel that my ability to hang in there when I don't really feel like it is one of the things that distinguishes me from others who may be more talented or clever. Sometimes you really have to hang on by your fingernails and tough it out.
>
> *Independent*, October 1990

Of the following list, then, not all are essential characteristics.

You may have hopeless communication skills, for instance, but if that is not a necessary quality to rise in your chosen field, or you can find someone who can communicate on your behalf, you can cover your weakness. I have met several senior executives who make presentations on behalf of the company because the chairman or chief executive doesn't enjoy doing it. But if you are after high status the following qualities are definite advantages:

Awareness of Rewards

There's no point running the race if you don't know where the finishing line is. The rewards will motivate you, be they fame, fortune, influence, satisfaction at helping others or a personal sense of achievement. The clearer you are about what rewards you are seeking, the better for you. You may need to conceal these from certain people because they may offend their values: some of us are put off by naked ambition or material greed. The 'how' of achievement is much easier to understand when we know 'why'. You don't want to end up like the disenchanted Harold Macmillan, who commented, 'Power? It's like a Dead Sea fruit; when you achieve it there's nothing there.'

Expectations of Success

Regard failure as feedback. Expectations of success are to do with self-image, with having a clear picture of your strengths and weaknesses and not being afraid to take risks.

Risk-taking

Top racing drivers, explorers and round-the-world yachtspeople might be addicted to risk. Our conditioning leads some of us to be frightened of taking risks. To become powerful we must be competitive, which brings with it the inevitable risk of failure.

Poor risks can be minimised by asking yourself:

- Have I got all the necessary information available to analyse this situation?

144

- What's the best that can happen if the risk pays off?

- What's the worst that can happen?

- Have I got the resources to deal with this?

- What can I do to make conditions as favourable as possible for success?

- Are there alternative courses of action to taking the risks?

- What happens if I do nothing? How do I think and feel about this?

Be selective about what issues you choose to take risks over, and don't rely too much on evidence from decisions you have taken in the past. The current circumstances could be very different. You may have lost money several years ago when you tried to get a similar project off the ground – perhaps your idea was ahead of its time. The questions above can have the word 'risk' replaced by 'decision' by those people who tend to procrastinate. As well as consideration of the pros and cons of a decision, pay attention to your intuition – it may have sensed something that your conscious mind is not aware of. Risk-taking makes us powerful because we act to control our fear.

Autonomy

High-status people are self-directing and determined. They will not be governed by high needs for approval and affection from others. They don't find it difficult to make decisions on their own and to get a sense of direction. They set clear objectives that they understand, sometimes with smaller goals on their way, and they convey these objectives clearly to people who can help them or whose help they need – unless, of course, they favour subterfuge (more about this on p. 150). Respect is more important to them than being regarded as endearing.

Opportunity-seeking

If you readily disclose what your aims are, people are more likely to provide you with opportunities. All too often we don't like to own up to ambition in case we fail. Using disclosure in conversation, too, will get other people to open up to you and often provide you with information about opportunities. Push yourself forward, volunteer for things, get trained and in touch with other people who are similarly motivated. If your boss leaves and the job's vacant, apply for it, even though you've only been with the company two years. People will start to see that you are keen on advancement.

Stamina

Physical and psychological fitness are helpful in the quest for status. Reputedly, Mother Teresa for instance sleeps for only four hours a night. You need to be able to work hard and long, and to cope with stress. Many of our former leaders on both sides of the Atlantic showed severe deterioration in health towards the end of their term of office – Ramsay MacDonald and Harold Macmillan in Britain, and Lyndon Johnson and Jimmy Carter in the USA are examples. We may not be aspiring to their lofty status; even so, we need to take care of ourselves to maintain our energy and clear thinking.

Ability to Pick People

You could be in a position to pick people to help you or to work for you. When you ask someone to help you, it's wise to choose someone who has decision-making power and real influence, rather than someone who only has title power. This is something to think about when you decide whether to take a job or not – association can be a powerful lever in gaining status, so if your boss does well and you work effectively together and are not perceived as a threat then your star may rise with hers or his.

Picking the right people to work for you so that you can delegate confidently is a great skill. You do not need to admire them or even like them, though it does help. It's a question of fitting the right face to the right role. An ambitious schemer, for instance, who could cause havoc in terms of office politics, may be ideal for masterminding methods of dealing with your company's main competitor.

When I was studying for my master's degree, I did a piece of research into the music business. This involved me talking to several people who had been employees of Richard Branson. They all, without exception, commented on his skill in picking excellent people to work alongside him.

Innovation

An ability to think creatively and to introduce new ideas is another attribute of powerful people. This is a talent that very often requires other skills to make the ideas come to practical fruition and to make them marketable. You may need to find a partner or adviser whom you can trust with your ideas – someone who has good business sense. To maintain status as an innovator, you need to keep up with the times and trends – unless, of course, you're lucky enough to make so much money out of early innovations that you can write books about them, go on chat shows, do a lecture tour or act as a consultant.

Projecting the Right Image

Journalists predicted that having overdosed on 'style' in the 1980s we would become much more 'content-conscious' in the 1990s. Does that mean we should now expect less contrived images of the famous? I doubt it. Integrity, ability, values, intellect and skills matter greatly, but we must consider the extent to which we respond to one another based on how we look, speak and behave. Your packaging needs to match the expectations that people have of you and your reputation – or dramatically contradict them so that you create news. The ability to communicate and represent yourself, your company or your cause appropriately is a great advantage.

Humour

A sense of humour is very useful in keeping a perspective on power. It can help you stop taking yourself, or the barbs of others who resent your success, quite so seriously. It can help you deal with the power games that are played all the time (see Chapter Three). It can be a great leveller and can show that you are human. Finally a sense of humour can help you shrug off failure.

DEALING WITH POWER-CONSCIOUS PEOPLE

In Chapters Four and Eight I talked about the difference between overt and active power. In an ideal world, as often described by books of this type, we would not have to deal with power-conscious people. They would be nurturing, encouraging and helpful, able to preserve their superiority and power without regarding those below them as a threat. Unfortunately, though, that is not the way the world really is. We all have status needs, and some of us who are insecure about having these needs met need a great deal of recognition and attention from others. We may do this by being pompous and self-important, by blocking others and being over-formal. We may be remote and inaccessible, tyrannical and temperamental. Rather than asserting our status through our skills, abilities and personal power, we will use it to make life as difficult as we can for others.

Businesses and other organisations are increasingly being restructured to create what's been called a 'flat hierarchy'. Your role in the company is clearly defined, but your development and the potential of the job are not blocked by bureaucracy. You are encouraged to become 'empowered'. Companies like Prudential Insurance, for instance, which used to have five graded dining rooms, now have just one and everyone is on Christian name terms. Businesses are starting to realise that 'empty suits' – bureaucrats who have little function and whose main purpose is to preserve overt power – are detrimental to success. Forward-thinking businesses have realised the crucial difference between overt and active power.

Does this mean that, with a change in approach to business, difficult, power-conscious people will disappear? Unfortunately not. There will always be a need to deal with people who are not really personally powerful and who feel they need to make strong use of authority and overt status to control others. Though the suggestions contained in this section are particularly relevant to dealing with this type of person, some of them are useful whenever you have to make a case for yourself, however receptive the listener. And although the examples throughout this section relate to dealing with power-conscious people at work, a lot of the suggestions work very well in other situations. The self-important teacher who complains about your child's behaviour, the officious doorman and the sneering shop assistant can all be dealt with using some of the tips in this section.

It's most important to remember that people who constantly assert their overt power are doing it because they have doubts about their real power. They need to make a show of their power to hire and fire, their company car or their inaccessibility to convince themselves as well as everyone else that they are important. They may insist you call them by their title and surname rather than their Christian name because it's respectful – it also keeps you at a safe distance. In some companies there are clear delineations of rank in terms of title – management are known by their titles and workers by their Christian names. I have run company courses on making tannoy announcements and telephone technique, where the audience included both workers and their supervisors; the workers have introduced themselves by their Christian names, while the supervisors used their titles and insisted on that form of address throughout the extremely informal training programme.

Get your attitude together towards these people. An ex-public schoolboy may have been brought up to believe that we're still in the days of the British Empire and that he has the right to inherit the world, but you've got the nous to know otherwise. He doesn't understand what's going on. Power-conscious players only have overt power claims over you. Nothing else. You can only allow people to make you feel inferior by your own consent.

Some of the following suggestions may be regarded as Machiavellian and manipulative. They are. You don't have to use them if they offend your sense of morality. It's just that sometimes when you're in a corner you need to fight dirty. I leave it to your own judgement. Deal with these difficult people through:

Making Them Feel Important

As you've identified this as a prime motive for their behaviour, it's useful to stroke their egos. This dosen't mean that you make yourself into a doormat, but that you outwit and disarm them in your use of tactics. These are:

- Asking them for help and advice, in a manner that says you expect they will be able to supply it. Don't grovel or be apologetic, but let them know that you are aware they are in a position to help you. If you can't think of any help or advice that you want, you could ask them a question to which you already know the answer – feigning gratitude and interest. Do this only if you trust your acting ability; the flattery value is well worth it.

- Thanking them for advice and help that they've given in the past. These people need acknowledgement: 'Thanks for the suggestion you made about the report. It really was very useful. I wonder if I could ask your advice about something else. I think I'm due for a pay rise. . . .'

- Letting them know you respect their expertise. 'I'm well aware that you know a lot about the pay structure in this company. . . .'

- Giving them proposals or suggestions they can alter. When we get involved with something, we start to take ownership of it – we get a sense of its starting to belong to us. Power players are keen on ownership. So rather than 'I've put down on paper what I think I should be earning', use the 'I've put down a range of ways in which I think my salary could be increased. Their are some gaps, though. Do you by any chance have some time to look over it, make whatever alterations are necessary and tell me what you think?'

- Giving them a good press. Tell other people how helpful they've been to you, so that it gets back to them. For instance, tell their opposite number in another department how useful they've been to you with your pay problem. You never know – this could be a self-fulfilling prophecy! And if the difficult person hears reports that they've been considered helpful, they may start genuinely to build on this. Let them hear you describe them in respectful tones as 'terribly busy' on the phone or that they're unavailable because they're going to Tokyo later on that day. Act as their public relations adviser, creating that reputation they so wish they had. In this role you are on your way to:

Making Yourself Indispensable

In doing this, you build up your power base. Get specialised knowledge of something at work – being the only person who understands the computer is a good one, and when you're absent you'll be well and truly missed. In a secretarial or personal assistant role, take over as much planning of your boss's life as you can. Run their diary, fix up theatre and opera tickets for them, keep time wasters away from them. Prioritise meetings and matters for their attention. Manage their time for them – and, who knows, they may find they can't function without you.

Become a source of information for them. One of the great fears that gnaws away at people who are conscious of their high status is that they may be conspired against and stabbed in the back. Keep your 'difficult person' as informed as possible about what is going on – unless, of course, you are involved in conspiracy yourself. Let them know when problems are starting to develop, rather than when the problem has become a large and difficult one to solve. How far you go with this tactic depends on how much allegiance you feel to other people. There's a fine line between discreet leaking of information and being a 'grass'.

If there is another 'difficult person' in the office whom the high-status player can't deal with, you may want to form an alliance. The latter may then regard you as essential in helping maintain some harmony at work.

Becoming a Skilled Negotiator

In Chapter Two I considered approaches to influencing: using Push, Pull and Exit strategies. The approaches described provide useful guidelines for negotiation. When you're dealing with high-power play, too much push won't work – you have to be a bit more subtle. The ideal outcome to a negotiation is a 'win-win' situation, where both parties think that they've gained something. In dealing with difficult people, you may want to plan on the premise that the outcome as far as they are concerned has to be one where they win and feel that they have the upper hand. You will find it useful to:

- Establish exactly what power resources you have in the situation. If you're a subordinate, these may not be very obvious. Do you have the ear of other influential people in the company? Can you incite your peers to rebellion? How much does your boss rely on you? Can you insinuate that you will withdraw support? What do you give your boss? You are going to use these resources to bargain with. Going back to the pay settlement situation, for instance, you could let your boss know that:

  – you've been talking to another senior manager about the prob-

lem (sub-text: 'And it could damage your reputation if I do this again').
- That there have been some other mutterings about pay rises among your colleagues (sub-text: 'Settle with me and I'll shut up and won't seek support from others').
- That you've been looking at your job description and have realised that in many ways you're taking a lot more responsibility than is stipulated (sub-text: 'And I'll stop doing this if you don't pay up').

It's important, too, for you to be very clear about what rewards and punishments you can use, even though you may be presenting them very indirectly.

- Remember you are bargaining – you want something that the other person can give, and they in return need something from you. You may need to spell out what they will get in return – improved performance, more commitment from you, you'll take on specific responsibilities. If you've just completed a successful project, won praise for an achievement of some description, or got your MBA, so much the better. If you're really scheming, you might want to do the difficult person a favour a few days before the negotiation so that they could already feel that they owe you something and are well-disposed towards you. Make sure your tactics aren't too transparent though. Have a 'fall-back' position for yourself – the absolute minimum you will accept. Keep this to yourself, though.

- Go in higher than you are aiming for. How this works is that you make your first high claim (for a £5000 pay rise, say), giving sound reasons why you want it. The high-power player explodes. Very reasonably, you say that you'll go and have a rethink. During the following week you run a campaign showing how valuable you are, solving problems for your boss, being extra charming to clients, taking a day off ill when you're really needed so that everything descends into disorder. Arrange for some campaign PR – get an ally to let the boss know that someone else has made you a job offer, or that you've been of invaluable assistance on something they've been working on. Be subtle about these tactics – you don't want to antagonise the difficult person by insulting their intelligence. Towards the end of your campaign arrange a second meeting to discuss the matter.

Choose a time when you know your boss will be at his or her most receptive – ten minutes before lunch or at the close of business is not a good idea. Go in and explain that after some consideration you've decided to ask for a lower amount (£4000) and what do they think. Both figures should be above your fall-back position.

- Make them think they provide the solution. Remember: high-status people like solving problems – it makes them feel import-ant. You may be able to present your case as a problem that poor old little you is incapable of solving. You need £30,000 a year to reflect your capabilities – it's what you would get elsewhere, and it's what you require to maintain your quality of life and per-formance in the job. It would make you very sad to go elsewhere to get this amount. Can they help you find a solution? What figure can they suggest?

- Recognise their difficulties. Let them know you appreciate that the current climate is difficult, that they've had to make cutbacks, that they're under a lot of pressure to increase productivity.

- Avoid getting entrenched in one issue. Look at the sideways options. You may think it's high time you were given a £5000 pay rise, to £30,000. Your boss may say it's out of the question. Are there other ways in which your needs can be met? Could you be given a company car, for instance? Move on to a four-day week? Have some performance-related bonuses? Be paid for by the company to do some part-time study? You always need to think about other options you can pursue, especially when your request meets with a definite refusal. Talking about these other options can also take the heat out of the debate. The more choice you give the high-status player to consider, the better.

- Present your case in a positive way. Contrast the following:
    'I really think I should be paid more. I could get a lot more elsewhere and I'm not getting the salary that reflects my abili-ties or performance. The project's going really well and we're going to be finished on deadline – it's made me realise how little I'm valued by this company. I don't know what you think. . . .'
  with
    'The project's going really well and I'm pleased to say we're going to be finished on deadline. I think it's going to give the

company's reputation a big boost. It's made me think about my value to the company. I think I'm worth more than I'm getting and that there's scope for a more realistic reflection of my abilities and performance. What d'you think?

The second example starts on a positive note and throughout makes much use of the positive. Whenever you're asking for anything follow a formula: positive, then negative. When you start off with the negative, the other person is more likely to respond emotionally and to start constructing defences and counter-arguments. It's likely they'll never hear the positive. Another formula which works well is the 'sandwich' one – open with something positive, put the unpalatable message in the middle and then end on a positive. Whingeing is a turn-off to most people, whether they are high-status players or not.

Don't be too self-important in the presentation of your case. This is a quality the high-power player knows well, and when they see it in others they recognise it as a threat. Don't appear over-preoccupied with your own significance or the importance of your job. See your job as part of the whole, contributing to the good of the company. The high-power player who appreciates bureaucracy will support this angle.

Try not to offer just two alternatives. It implies limitation of choice to the high-status person, and a scant investigation of options on your behalf. When presented with just two options the high-status player will often look for a third themselves – and of course it could be 'fire 'em'. . . . Rather than 'I'd like a pay rise, or I'll have to think about moving on', go for 'I'd like a pay rise or some sponsored training, or I'll have to think about moving.'

When we are offering options we tend to put the option we really want first. It's always better to offer the positive at the outset. When the options are not clearly negative and positive you may want to throw the other party off the scent, by putting what you really want last. This is useful if the other party is very difficult and always tends to go against the wishes of others. So for instance if you really want to get a company car, use the following order: 'So are we saying then that the options are sponsored training, performance related benefits or a company car?'

- Give the high-power players plenty of airtime. The more you listen to their viewpoint, the more you can calculate how you can angle your case to appeal to their needs. Use the 'Exit' technique to go away and think about what you've heard and to plan your next move. Talking at a high-power player rarely works – they know that tactic, because they usually use it themselves.

Considering Their Aspirations and Fears

Analyse what motivates the high-power player and what they are afraid of. If they like formality, then use it yourself; informality and spontaneity may be threatening to them and may make them more resistant to your case. So if you're after more money, prepare something on paper for them to look over beforehand. If you know that they are concerned about their reputation, use this as a bargaining tool – can you offer to do something, such as run a project that would make them look good? If they value hard work and let it be known that they work longer hours than everyone else, then be seen to be working late the odd evening. Try and see how what you do fits in with their goals.

If they rely on their strong personalities to maintain high-power play, creating dependency on others, remember that you can show strength by appearing independent. If they rely heavily on their expert power, there is always a risk that someone else will be a greater expert or that their knowledge can be out-of-date. Make a point of showing that you can use the qualities they value – aggressively opinionated types often don't like 'yes' people and regard them with contempt. John Major is said to have come to Margaret Thatcher's attention through vigorous argument against a case that she was championing. Through his stand, he indicated he was 'one of us'.

Appeal to aspiration by emphasising how rare and exclusive something is. When something is unique, or there are very few of them and they are very much in demand, their value increases dramatically. It may need subtly pointing out that you are the only person in the office who understands the workings of every piece of software on your system, for instance. Taking another example, if you are trying to persuade the high-power player to buy something or invest some money in training, pointing out that the something is the only one available or that the training is exclusive and creates specialists can work very well.

Use language that appeals to their values. If they resist innovation and change, because it is threatening to their position, try and put the case for a 'traditional' approach, a 'tried and tested' method and 'reliability'. If they pride themselves on their common sense, talk of 'realistic', 'practical' and 'cost-effective' measures.

Putting the Pressure On

You may have to resort to pressure tactics. These include forming allies, getting the ear of an equally influential person of similar standing and forcing decisions through applying pressures of time, money and fear. For example, 'I would like your decision about this matter by next Monday. I have been offered another job and they need a decision by Tuesday.' The more the pressure the greater the stress, and under stress choices become reduced. But when using pressure, be aware that the decision reached may be a more extreme one and may not necessarily go in your favour.

Analysing the Situation

When problems arise it is better to tackle them one by one, rather than letting them mount up. The same goes for getting your ideas accepted or expressing disagreement – do it gradually, issue by issue. Here are some questions to answer that can lead you to solutions for handling difficult power-conscious people:

- What is the specific situation that I want to resolve?
- How do I think the difficult person regards me?
- How do I regard them?
- What is my behaviour like towards them?
- What do I need? What have they got?
- What have I got? What do they need?
- How could our relationship be improved?
- What is the least that I am prepared to accept?
- What would be the best?
- What practical steps can I use to go about solving this problem?

Dealing with Conflict

If all else fails, remember the following:

- Establish clearly what you want and need.

- If the high-power player starts attacking you verbally or changing the subject use the 'broken record' technique, repeating your main demand.

- Avoid personal criticism of the other party or making it all their fault. Apportioning blame usually meets with justification as defence, and the situation gets nowhere. Take responsibility. It's the difference between 'and you should have . . . ' and 'it would have been better if we'd. . . .'

- Keep your behaviour under control. It's very useful to disclose your feelings ('I feel angry/hurt/upset'), but do it in a calm, collected way. Difficult people often seek to control more than is appropriate, to the detriment of others: don't give them the satisfaction of seeing you lose control. Vent your anger or frustration when you leave the room. Beat up a cushion.

- If you are criticised, use an assertiveness technique called 'fogging'. Thank your opponent for the criticism and do not question it further or attempt to justify it:

    Critic: I'm sorry, but you were just not very competent over that project.
    You: Oh, that's useful to know. I'm glad at least to have the feedback.

    This sabotages the offensive most effectively – though you risk being regarded as defiant.

- The participative approach as described in Chapter Two is very useful. Use the 'Exit' door if you've caught the difficult person on a bad day or at a bad time.

- Another assertiveness technique can help pre-empt criticism. If you suspect you are about to be criticised over something or that the other person is nursing some grievances, acknowledge it: 'I know you were unhappy about the way I ran the team towards the end of last year . . . ' or 'I know my work's not been up to scratch recently. . . .'

- If at all possible, try and leave the situation on a civilised even if not positive note. Be courteous and thank them for their time. Unclench those teeth.

RESPONSIBILITIES OF POWER

Once you've got status, you may find yourself faced with new responsibilities. You will find yourself in the position, perhaps, of having to use authority, develop and discipline people, build teams and live up to a reputation. You could find that you need to:

Delegate

If you've always carried most of the responsibility yourself, this function can take some adjusting to. Remember that one of the most frustrating aspects of a job can be 'role underload', and that if people are not encouraged to take responsibility they will not develop and so lack of job satisfaction may cause them to leave. With involvement, people get a sense of ownership. Start by delegating those tasks that are low priorities and take up too much of your time – those tasks that other people can perform as well as, if not better than, you can. Choose people who will be able to do the task well and who will feel enthusiasm towards it. You may need to create enthusiasm. Brief the person clearly on the task, let everyone else know that they are doing it and why, and make yourself accessible to monitor progress. Communicate praise for the job when it is done effectively – in front of others, if possible.

Criticise

To develop other people and maintain standards you need to be able to criticise constructively. Give criticism as soon after the event as you can. Make sure that you know why you want to give it and what exactly you want to criticise. There is no point criticising behaviour or situations that cannot be changed. Think in terms of action – what could be done – rather than descriptive adjectives. It's the difference between 'perhaps you could have reassured them more' and 'perhaps you could have been more confident'.

Let the person know that you are giving your opinion – 'I think', 'It's my opinion that' – rather than speaking as the voice of God. Be as specific as you can, and use sufficient explanation to amplify understanding. Rather than relating a catalogue of wrongdoings, keep your negative points to a maximum of two. Ask the other person questions to clarify that they understand what you are saying and are not getting upset. The golden rule of criticism, which makes all the difference to the way it is taken, is to start with a positive comment, then to give the criticism. We hear the positive and it cushions us for the negative. We feel we are being given a balanced appraisal.

If you have designated the task that is under criticism, check that you explained it adequately and that you do not have a personal agenda against the person concerned.

Build Teams

As team leader it is your responsibility to set an example. Communication between you and your team members and among them is very important. You need to keep to agreements you make with people and not shy away from conflict in groups, which is natural, but work quickly to resolve it. The team needs goals and direction, which need to be clearly communicated. Members need individual consideration and attention; some may need training to meet the requirements of the job, and coaching and counselling when they have problems. The team is a delicate balance of individuals' needs being met and collective spirit; team leaders need to encourage members to support one another, to tackle problems together and to work towards common benefits.

Network

It can be lonely at the top. A rise in status may make you feel isolated and believe that others resent your success. You may need to look for new sources of support and alliance. If this is the case seek out networks you can join, both formal and informal. Are there other people at your level whom you can call for advice and perhaps meet socially? Networks serve as exchanges for ideas and contacts; they also function as lobbying groups which champion causes.

Mentor

Mentors serve as guides to others, offering information, support and advice. Some organisations foster formal mentoring. As mentor you may find yourself offering advice on company politics, career progress, confidence-building and emotional matters. It can be a rewarding experience to see your protégé develop, and also very gratifying for your ego.

When you act as a role model you serve as an example for others to follow. It's my view that we should act as role models with care. In attracting so much aspiration and setting an example, we can appeal to those who lack self-possession and aggravate this deficiency rather than easing it. We can explain to those who are using us as role models that there are approaches and behaviour we use that are worth studying. We should emphasise though, that we are not gods, and that it is their own individuality that they should prize above all else. In giving people heroine or hero status, we inevitably diminish our own.

Phew, high power sounds like hard work! If you're finding it to be so, take time to reassess and ask yourself two questions:

- Am I still enjoying this?
- Am I still learning?

chapter seven

PERSONAL POWER SKILLS: BEHAVIOUR, VOICE AND APPEARANCE

Personal power skills are to do with matching your style of presentation to your substance. This chapter deals with the way we can use non-verbal signals and appearance to convey significance. It covers body language, the speaking voice and clothing signals. My previous book, *Your Total Image*, investigated these aspects in detail. Here we look at how we can use these presentation skills specifically to develop personal power and to gain recognition from others.

The appropriate use of these signals cannot be over-estimated. However skilled you are at putting your case verbally, the way you look and sound indicates to others how they should respond to you. 'Language', said Samuel Johnson, 'is the dress of thought'; when we misunderstand or mistrust what language conveys, then we rely on the other signals to supply us with meaning. You may know and use every assertiveness technique going – but if you don't match your message by looking and sounding assertive, then using the techniques in isolation will be of little use.

It's widely recognised that first impressions matter. We use judgement based on these first impressions to enable us to know how to communicate with one another. Few of us are free of irrational prejudice, ranging from aversions to suede shoes to wariness of others based on their race, gender, age or obvious sexual preferences. These prejudices may figure strongly in the way we initially assess one another.

The understanding of how people use these signals can be helpful in raising your personal power and in analysing and controlling your response to high-power play from others. When thinking about how you look and speak, and how you respond to others, the following points are worth remembering:

- Behaviour is highly contagious. Apologetic posture and incoherent mumbling will cause a reaction in others, as will a self-important swagger and a pompous, booming voice. By learning to control your own behaviour, when necessary, you can resist other people's attempts to dominate you. Watch how the skilled interviewee on television avoids being aroused by the machine gun tactics of the hounding interviewer.

- Behaviour and self-presentation are governed by habit. When someone moves and talks quickly and abruptly it could mean they are impatient or irritated – on the other hand, that could be their habitual style of moving and speaking. Habits can be changed and adapted.

- Improving the way you look and sound is to do with developing awareness and adaptability. Increasing your self-awareness is not the same as being preoccupied with yourself. Awareness can help you understand others better and make you more adaptable. Understanding and adaptability are indispensable qualities in raising your status.

  Some people are highly suspicious of any suggestions that they can change the way they behave. They argue that it's 'not natural'. But all of us have moulded, developed and disciplined what's 'natural' in order to adapt to and live in our society. Learning, building skills and acquiring culture are all to do with shaping the 'natural'. Consciously improving your speaking voice or use of body language is no more 'unnatural' than learning a foreign language. Changes in behaviour will only seem 'artificial' to others if the skills have not been understood, practised and absorbed.

- Other people do not necessarily mean what we would mean if we used the same signals. For instance, if you do not approve of something you may indicate this through showing very little reaction. Perhaps you assume that when others show little reaction they too are showing disapproval. It's worth considering that their behaviour is habitual, that their 'communicating style' is characterised by inexpressiveness, that they are what's been called 'low reactors'. We cannot assume that other people mean what we would mean were we sending the same signals.

- One-off instances of behaviour do not necessarily represent an important part of someone's personality. People have off-days, and if it's your bad luck to meet that person on the day they are sitting defensively and snapping abruptly at people that may only be an indication of their behaviour in a given situation. As a clue to their personality, repeated evidence of the same response is a better guide.

POWER AND BODY LANGUAGE

Appearances are not held to be a clue to the truth. But we seem to have no other.

Ivy Compton Burnett

Although outward appearance need not necessarily reflect an attitude, other people may perceive it to do so. Through our use of body language we can indicate to others how powerful we feel ourselves to be in a situation, and how much power we expect to be given by others. Personal power can be conveyed through:

Posture

Good posture not only makes you look better, it can also make you feel more energetic and purposeful. Attention to posture can help backache and poor breathing habits. Twenty years of habitual slumping, and your most frequently assumed position is inevitably going to be a slump. Others may regard you as having a depressed, defeated air.

It would be misleading to suggest that posture can be changed quickly and easily. The Alexander Technique, a corrective therapy to realign the body, works gently and slowly to replace bad habits.

Knotted muscles caused by tension can be alleviated through massage, aromatherapy, yoga and relaxation exercises. Some exercise systems, like Pilates for example, place great emphasis on postural improvement.

Even without outside help, you can improve your posture through reminding yourself frequently about it on a day-to-day basis and learning to relax tension spots. As you are working to counteract entrenched habits, quick reminders to yourself several times a day – when you're hunched over the phone, say, or scrunched up in a traffic jam – are better than spending an hour a week trying to do this. Use the following tips:

- The more conscious you become of lengthening out your spine when you sit and stand, the greater the benefit for your posture. Check that your energy is directed upwards, so that you feel suspended from the top of your head. Your spine should feel as long and wide as it can be.

- Relax the back of your neck and lengthen it out by nodding the head gently up and down. Roll the shoulders round in circles and then let them drop down and back.

- In a sitting position, make sure that the back of the chair supports the small of your back. When standing, think of your spine being as long as possible, your weight evenly distributed on both feet, with your knees slightly bent so that your buttocks tuck under.

Open Body Language

We can use body language to look confident and receptive or defensive and insecure. When a cat's really enjoying itself, it rolls around on the floor offering up its underbelly for stroking. Few of us regularly go that far – but when we feel at ease in a situation we tend to leave the front of our bodies more exposed. We don't need to protect the soft, fleshy, vulnerable parts from attack. So rather than wrapping your arms across your body and crossing your legs, convey confidence through a more open position, with arms by your side, hands folded in your lap and feet firmly on the ground.

You could take a tip from the royal family and some politicians, who are trained to use high-status body language. If your shoulders and arms are relaxed enough, let your arms hang loosely by your side – for a more formal appearance, let your arms hang loosely behind your back with your hands folded together. Keep your hands and arms away from your face – it's your best 'visual aid', and in concealing it you appear nervous, reluctant, dubious – even deceitful.

We often use closed body language to give ourselves reassurance in a situation. For instance, folded arms feel comfortable – as though a person's cuddling themselves. If you don't know what to do with your hands, then many body language experts recommend 'steepling' – that is, linking the fingers together. This works well when the hands are in the lap. In my experience, when people start talking and steepling their hands in front of their upper body and face it can look very contrived. If it feels natural for you to move your hands around when you talk, then do so.

Occupation of Space

Personal power is about feeling comfortable with being regarded as significant. Some people habitually use body language that makes them look physically smaller and apologises for their presence. Other people with naturally small physiques may habitually use body language that makes them look powerful and substantial. You can quickly see this for yourself in a mirror. Stand with your legs cros-sed, hands folded in front of your body in what's known as the 'fig-leaf' position, and tilt your head downwards. You'll see that you don't occupy much space. Now take a wider stance, put your hands on your hips and throw back your head – you'll see that you look significantly larger.

We use space and size to indicate power in terms of the houses and cars we buy, and we can use body language to do likewise. Be aware that when we're on our 'best behaviour' we tend to position ourselves symmetrically so that we look neat, tidy and contained. When we're more relaxed we take up more space through asym-metrical positioning, arms relaxing over the back of the chair, legs stretched out to the other side.

Look comfortable occupying space through sitting well back in your chair, resting your arms on the chair arms, or, if you're seated at a table or desk, steepling your hands together and resting your arms on the table – staking out some territory for yourself. When you're standing, if you want to look confident and powerful adopt an upright posture and position yourself so that you can be clearly seen; avoid protecting yourself behind chairs or tables, or hugging the wall or doorway.

Don't use body language as compensation for your physique. It will only draw attention to your size or lack of it. Some tall people, for instance, constantly stoop to get down to the level of the rest of us. Some small people may puff out their chests and pull back their heads to try and make themselves look physically larger.

You can occupy space and mark out territory through use of possessions. If you spread your papers, for instance, over a table at a meeting, you are extending your area of physical influence. But this can be taken too far: it's irritating and intrusive to have someone else pick up one of your possessions – say a pen – and start to fiddle with it.

Indicating Involvement and Detachment

Lean forward, craning your head towards the other person, and you send out signals that you are keen for involvement. Lean back in a chair, with your head tilting backwards and your hand covering your mouth, and you'll send out signals that you are detached from the situation. Some people habitually adopt the latter attitude as their means of 'getting by'. They sense that others interpret their apparent detachment to imply criticism and evaluation. They try to raise their own status through playing 'judge'. In fact this is very defensive behaviour. It suggests that the 'judge' finds involvement dangerous because, if she or he evaluates less and participates more, they become vulnerable. Good heavens – they could even be seen to make mistakes!

If you have to deal with someone who uses an aloof, detached attitude, asking them for a response ('What do you think of what I've said so far?', 'How do you feel that would work?') can encourage a response and help you know where you stand. In terms of body language, getting a physical response can also make this cool customer more involved. Show them a paper, proposal or article that they physically have to look over and comment on.

Positioning

You need to match your body language to your message, and to use it in a way that's appropriate to your personality and situation. If you are taking a forceful approach, for instance, and you know you have a tendency to allow others to dominate you, a more detached use of body language can help. When you find it difficult to get involved, positioning yourself so that you suggest you want to be in the midst of things is a good idea.

You can use body language to build rapport with others. We do this instinctively all the time. Therapists use it to build empathy with their clients. When you go in and see the managing director who assumes a detached attitude, and you lean forward in your chair making yourself look smaller, you are emphasising the difference between her or his dominance and your submissiveness. If a troubled subordinate comes to see you and looks defensive and apologetic, and you sit back looking expansive, the difference in the two attitudes is emphasised.

Where you sit and stand is also important. I've already mentioned how looking comfortable in open space can convey status. Sitting at the head of the table also confers power. The most confrontational position is one in which you sit or stand directly opposite the other person. Sitting at right-angles to one another helps build rapport.

Positioning is, of course, dependent on furniture and the environment. With a round table it's difficult to appear distinctively different unless you are separated from everyone else by having greater space on either side of your chair. With a rectangular table you are most involved when you sit at the centre of one of the long sides, and least involved at the end of the line. In my experience in training, people who least like being 'one of the crowd' very often sit at the end of a line. See Dr David Lewis's book *The Secret Language of Success* for further insights on positioning and the arrangement of furniture.

Control of Displacement Activity

Displacement activity is what we do to channel our tension. The description covers a wide variety of actions – chewing gum, twiddling hair, drumming fingers on a table, twitching the feet and rearranging clothing. For onlookers, displacement activity can be very distracting. Counteract excessive use of it by relaxing physically as much as you can before going into a situation – shaking out legs and arms, and easing tension from neck and shoulders.

Objects often become part of the displacement activity – a pen or notes acting as an effective 'security blanket'. In tense situations, some people find it useful to provide themselves with an object on which they can focus their tension. For instance, you could have a pebble in your pocket which you grip on to very firmly. Only you know it's there, and it acts as a diversion for the tension which might otherwise be expressed in a more distracting manner. To convey status, you want to look confident, relaxed but purposeful.

Control of Movement

When we are ill at ease in a situation, many of us use body language that reflects a stress response. We show our discomfort through behaviour that indicates we feel the need to 'fight or flee'. Fists can clench, jaws set, legs brace, chests puff out. Alternatively, we may find it difficult to stand still, our heads may pull back ready for 'lift off' and our arms may hang rigidly at our sides – we may give the impression that we are revving up on the runway to get away as soon as possible.

High status, indicating that you are comfortable and at ease in a situation, is characterised by relaxed stillness, with little distracting movement. Quick, jerky movement suggests that a person is under pressure. Orders and requests gain power when they are made with relatively little head movement. Great orators like Martin Luther King used the power of stillness to great advantage. If someone is pressuring you, slowing down your movement can help and prevent them forcing your hand.

Eye Contact

The making and breaking of eye contact is highly significant in transmitting power. Steady, sustained eye contact is very powerful and may be interpreted as aggressive. When you meet another person and your eyes meet, you indicate submissiveness if you break eye contact and then look back.

Extremes of holding eye contact, or failing to give any, can indicate that a person is trying to play high power. Not looking at another person at all can be the visual equivalent of 'sending them to Coventry', the power sub-text being they are not worthy of your attention or recognition. This is why shy people who sometimes find it difficult to make eye contact with others can be assessed as 'arrogant'.

It's unnatural and unnerving to stare relentlessly at other people. Our eyes reflect brain activity and move around as we think. To convey status and to show that you are considering others and their responses it's important to make good eye contact when you first meet other people and then to look at them frequently as you talk, checking their reactions and understanding. These looks should be long enough to acknowledge them as individuals (on courses, we tell people who have difficulties in this situation to say the other person's name silently to themselves as they look). If your glances are too short they may have an unsettling effect, and at worst make you look like a frightened rabbit.

For the self-effacing, it's important to make as much eye contact when you speak as you do when you listen. When talking to more than one person, you can raise your power by sharing eye contact with everyone. That way, you maximise your chances of influencing the whole group.

Many of us, when faced with someone who seems to be sending signals of disinterest or disapproval, will tend to avoid looking at the offending party. To gain power, increase the amount of eye contact you make with that person. They may be behaving in that manner because deep down inside they need attention. Rather than being discouraged by their show of self-importance, acknowledge their need for recognition and give them the power they crave. Few of us do this instinctively; it's a useful technique, especially when your objective is to influence or persuade. If you are on the receiving end of determined persuasion, then focusing your eyes away from the person's gaze to an object, their feet or your watch can help end the assault.

Facial Expression

The bottom half of the face is as important in conveying confidence and comfort in a situation as is the use of eye contact. The jaw and mouth are common sites of tension, and can indicate to others that you feel nervous and insecure. The more relaxed the muscles, the more responsive your facial expression will be to the impression you wish to create. In negotiating, inscrutability can be useful; but in meetings, presentations and interviews we want to keep people listening, and an animated face with changing facial expression can be one of the most useful tools in doing this. We tend to trust people more when they show facial expression, too. Your facial expression tells others how they should respond to you; if you think your use of it could be more flexible, do the exercises on p. 174.

Touch

When we use body language mannerisms that involve touching ourselves, such as patting hair, rubbing arms and legs or adjusting clothes, these gestures serve as reassurance. In Chapter Three I mentioned how giving verbal reassurance can serve as high-power play. Touching another person on the arm or back as comfort can serve the same function. You assume a degree of intimacy and say 'There, there' in the way that adults do to children. So initiating touch can be regarded as powerful, though it may also be interpreted as patronising. In a first meeting, you raise your power by being the first person to proffer your hand to the other.

THE SOUND OF STATUS: YOUR SPEAKING VOICE

Mr Major spoke with more confidence and conviction than ever before. The voice lessons he spurned three years ago (when I and others gingerly suggested them to him) as unnecessary confection have been undertaken at last, with demonstrable results: his delivery is stronger, deeper, more authoritative.

Andrew Neil, writing in the *Sunday Times*, October 1995.

A controlled, confident tone of voice is a valuable asset in communicating power. When other people like the way you sound, they will listen far more readily to what you have to say. And it's easier to achieve than many people realise. Here are some practical suggestions for conveying power through:

Breath Control

Your use of breath provides the basic power for your voice. When you control your breath efficiently you gain control over volume and pitch. In addition, good breath control can help control stress and make you feel much more in control.

We're often advised, when faced with a difficult task or situation, to 'take a deep breath in'. This can lead to poor breathing patterns – excessive effort being used for inspiration and holding of the breath, so that when it's exhaled the sound comes out in a breathy, uncontrolled stream. And extra oxygen you've taken in may make you feel light-headed and panicky. So forget taking a deep breath in, and when you need to make an effort tell yourself instead to 'take a slow breath out'. This way you control the increase in rate of respiration that occurs as a result of stress. Our bodies often perform this response automatically – as when we sigh or yawn, for instance.

To breathe efficiently, you need to get maximum use of the bottom part of your pear-shaped lungs. When you breathe in, there should be little audible sound and you should be able to feel your stomach muscles releasing outwards as the dome-shaped diaphragm beneath the lungs drops downwards. Your ribs should swing outwards. As you breathe out, you should be able to feel your stomach muscles flattening as the diaphragm rises upwards. Think about breathing from the belly: breathe in, stomach out; breathe out, stomach in.

To develop better breath control spend a few minutes every day, first thing in the morning or last thing at night (lying on your back in bed is a good place to do this), just focusing on your breathing with a hand placed on your stomach. Breathe easily, and each time you take a gentle breath in extend the out breath. Count one on the first out breath, two on the second, and so on until you build up to about seven or eight. Check that your body is relaxed and your neck and shoulders are free of tension (see p. 164).

Put good breathing habits into practice in everyday situations. When you rush to pick up the phone, for instance, rather than snatching in a quick breath, breathe out slowly. When you launch into a proposal or a case, prepare yourself by taking a few slow, controlled breaths *out* rather than gulping large amounts of unnecessary air *in*.

Good breath control is invaluable for feeling and sounding in control:

> There is no food or vitamin pill in the world that can do for you what excellent breathing patterns can do.
>
> Anthony Robbins, *Unlimited Power*

Pace

Like physical movement, a quick, jerky pace will suggest that you don't enjoy holding the floor, that you're nervous, that you don't feel you've got the right to hog the airtime. Pace is about rate of delivery – that is, how many words come out of the mouth a minute (on average 130) and the use of pause. It's better to err towards a rapid rate of delivery than a slow one – you will sound quick-thinking rather than ponderously pompous. To keep people listening, to encourage them to absorb what you are saying, to give yourself time to recover and prepare physically and mentally for what you are going to say next and to consider the reactions of your listeners, you need to make good use of pause.

In communicating power, pause is the auditory equivalent of physical stillness. Uncomfortable with using pause, you may fill the gaps with 'ums' and 'ers'. Practise talking or reading and mentally tell yourself, when you pause, 'I pause and I breathe'. Be aware that the breath drops to the bottom of your lungs easily as your stomach releases out, and that once you've recharged you can continue. Don't be affected by other people's behaviour: when someone is firing questions with a shotgun delivery, pause and breathe before you answer. They may want to operate under pressure, but you don't have to succumb to their tactics. If you choose to, you can withstand their pressure by giving yourself recovery time before you speak.

Vary your pause to suit your purpose and to keep people listening to you. If you want to motivate and inspire people, there needs to be a sense of mission and enthusiasm behind your message. Move on with the pace. If you need to convey authority and reassurance, your delivery will benefit from being less hurried. Play around with a good tape recorder to get variety. When you're trying for variety ask people you trust for feedback: 'Am I going too quickly?' or 'Would you like me to get a move on here?'

Nervousness causes many people to talk too quickly. But in my opinion it's preferable to talking too slowly and thereby insulting your listeners' intelligence. Effective use of pause enables you to evaluate how your message is being received, and whether you should edit it or change tack. In making appropriate use of pause, you will be heard to take control of other people's time and your own. This is using your personal power.

Pitch

The pitch of your voice can reflect how relaxed or tense you are in a situation. High-pitched voices travel further, as the notes have a higher frequency. To hear if you confuse pitch and volume, count from one to ten, starting very quietly and getting louder. Listen to your voice to hear if the pitch has risen too. To train yourself to distinguish between the two, alternate counting from one to ten, first increasing the volume and then raising the pitch.

Your pitch may rise uncontrollably because of inadequate breath control or throat tension. Check that you are breathing efficiently and that your neck and throat are relaxed. Nod your head gently, and see if you can talk at the same time without tensing your neck. Practise your breath control, letting the breath drop low into the lungs and then sighing and yawning as you breathe out. Both activities are excellent for relaxing the throat.

When we speak we use pitch patterns. An upward inflection conveys a very different message from a downward one. Say 'I'd need you to do that for me' using a rise in pitch at the end, and contrast it with a downward fall at the end. If you have difficulty hearing pitch, use a finger like a baton to conduct yourself – lifting it as you rise in pitch, and lowering it as you fall. You'll hear that in the first instance the request sounds tentative and open to negotiation; in the second it sounds resolved and definite.

You can use pitch, then, to reinforce your message. If you tend to come over as bombastic, play around with using pitch rises more frequently – making your recommendations sound more like suggestions. Rather than alienating people through instructing them what to do, you will appeal to their intelligence and powers of discrimination. If you find that your pitch rises a great deal, or you lack a definite, decisive tone, play around with using pitch falls.

Adopting a strong falling pattern when you are challenged or uncertain can give you a confident tone.

Projection and Clarity

We tend to associate confidence and presence with clear, audible voices. Adequate breath control is again important: professional voice users like opera singers and actors spend years exercising so that they build up their breath capacity. As we hear our own voices through bone conduction in our heads, rather than as others hear them, it can be difficult to estimate just how much volume you are using.

To speak loudly and clearly your speech organs – jaw, tongue, teeth and lips – need to be relaxed and mobile. Earlier in this chapter I mentioned facial expression. If your facial muscles are tense and immobile, it's unlikely that you will be able to project your voice to its full capacity. You may sound as though you speak through clenched teeth – not an effect that encourages other people to behave receptively back to you. Learn to relax the muscles by releasing the jaw and yawning, stretching the lips forwards and backwards, and chewing vigorously. Remember that we lip-read one another, and that very often poor projection is down to a reluctance to use much energy in the muscles of the lips. Practise reading and talking while exaggerating your articulation wildly, then check in the mirror to lessen the exaggeration until it looks acceptable.

The above exercise can also help with clarity. Clear speech is important, because many people unconsciously make a connection between clarity of speech and clarity of thinking. If you tend to miss out letters, to some ears it can sound like the auditory equivalent of very scruffy clothes. They may confuse your speech with your personality, and assume that like your style of speaking you are slap-dash and pay little attention to detail.

When you're working on projection and clarity, check that you are making sufficient eye contact to see exactly where you want to send the sound. Ask people whether they can hear you. To keep people listening we need to vary volume, and often the most significant thing you say can be best delivered by using a quiet, confiding tone rather than a declamatory blast. For a short while, people will listen a little harder. When several people are talking at once, or you want to make yourself heard above a lot of distraction, persist in talking quietly and relentlessly and you will eventually be heard.

Accent

In Britain, the subject of accent is still a hot potato. Depending on our prejudices, we ascribe social standing to people according to their accents. The 'right on' punk violinist may accentuate a Cockney twang to increase his 'street cred'; the aspiring Conservative politician may make a determined effort to round his or her vowels so that they carry greater appeal for the blue-rinse brigade.

Some people adapt their accents very quickly, showing a keen ear and a strong desire to fit in and be acceptable. In some circumstances this can be a pragmatic tactic. A friend who has a very successful career in the hotel business realised when he started work at the Savoy that his prospects were limited by his broad Midlands accent. He spent every available moment listening to Radio Four, studying how the announcers spoke. His accent is still audible, but he now sounds what some people would describe as 'educated' and 'cultured'. He has no qualms whatsoever about the adaptations he has made. He believes they were necessary for him to achieve his goals.

Whatever your accent, you can have a good speaking voice. If you are troubled by the response people make to your accent, then before doing something about it check that it's not the other person's problem. They may be ribbing you as the only means available of asserting their superiority. Perhaps they are threatened by nonconformity. If your accent is preventing you being understood by others, then you can 'clean it up'. Listen to the sounds you make that deviate most widely from standard speech. In a Welsh accent, for instance, one of the sounds would be 'eeuuuur' or 'heeaa' for 'here'. In Liverpudlian it would be 'fur her' for 'fair hair'. Select at most three or four of these sounds and proceed to work on their pronunciation until they become more readily understood. Record a friend who makes these sounds in standard fashion and listen to and imitate their pronunciation. You may want to buy a simple speech exercise book which repeats certain sounds and shows you where they are made in the mouth. Remember, too, that you may be more readily understood through easing up on the pace and sharpening up your articulation.

I think people should be proud of their accents and their roots, which add distinction and colour to our cultural life. Britain would be a much duller-sounding land if everyone spoke the same way. Very often, people who complain about their own accents can get to like their speaking voices through some attention to breath control, pace, pitch and projection.

PERSONAL POWER AND CLOTHING

It's a mass-produced symbol of my individuality and belief in personal freedom.
Sailor talking about his snakeskin jacket, in David Lynch's
Wild at Heart

Clothes and grooming signals transmit power. We expect female royals, film stars and popes to deck themselves out in rich colours and opulent fabrics. Their appearances yell: 'I am significant.' Fashion trends used to start with the upper classes; haute couture still influences high street fashion, but these days 'street cred' styles like punk and hip-hop create trends, too.

The history of status and clothing is a fascinating one. Clothes act as a barometer of social change; one of the most dramatic examples was the change in women's clothing that occurred after the First World War. Pre-war Edwardian women wore heavy, constricting clothes emphasising their status as decorative objects and wives. During the war, because the men were away fighting many women had to work in areas like munitions, and in clothing practicality became much more important. After the war, when there was a shortage of men and some women had been given the vote, the role of the single working woman in society began to be accepted. In the 1920s, women started to cut their hair short and to wear simple shift dresses. See *Understanding Fashion* by Elizabeth Rouse for a full history of the links between status and fashion.

Today, women and men have a great deal of choice over what they wear. Women have a greater range of colours and shapes to choose from, and they are still expected to fulfil a decorative function. Leading statesmen and male politicians adopt a sombre, earnest style of dressing. The few female luminaries that we see tend to go for a much more flamboyant look. Margaret Thatcher was as colourful as John Major is drab: she emphasised her prominence through her clothes. In this final section, I want to look at the personal power messages that both sexes convey through appearance. Power can be conveyed through:

Size Signals

Clothes can make us look bigger or smaller, and emphasise certain parts of the body. Power dressing for both sexes emphasised the shoulders, suggesting plenty of scope for 'shouldering responsibility'. Women looked more predatory with long nails and high heels. 'Power hair' – lots of it, piled high to make the head look bigger (which photographs better because the body looks comparatively smaller) – is still fashionable. It's become less disciplined, though – Ivana Trump's and Fergie's beehives look a lot less sculpted than hairstyles did ten years ago.

Like expansive body language, clothes can make you appear more significant. Warm, bright colours 'advance' towards the eye of onlookers and stand out from the crowd. Large patterns and shiny material can make people look conspicuously larger than they are. Physical smallness will be emphasised by wearing large, loose garments, bulk emphasised by encasing the body in tight-fitting garments. It all depends on where the eye is drawn to, and comparisons between the wearer and the garment's size: a boxy, double-breasted jacket will make the wearer look 'squarer' – fine if you're a tall person, but if you're small and skinny then the comparison will emphasise your diminutive frame. A plumper person will appear slimmer in a single-breasted jacket – the shape forming a single vertical line through the centre of the body and drawing an onlooker's eye to this.

Well-cut clothes in which the wearer feels and looks comfortable will convey that she or he has 'the measure of themselves'. It's worth getting clothes altered, and if in doubt always buy on the large side to make this possible.

Apparent Affluence

Clothes are indicators of 'conspicuous consumption'. Bespoke tailoring, cashmere, metres and metres of suede and leather can show that the wearer has money to spend on appearance. Wealth, of course, doesn't buy taste – a quick stroll around Bond Street, Knightsbridge or Fifth Avenue will demonstrate that. With less of it around, it's become less fashionable to dress to 'flash the cash'. On a budget you can still convey apparent affluence through prioritising what you spend your money on. For instance:

- You wear a good haircut twenty-four hours a day, every day. If you can spare the time, several top hairdressers have training schools where supervised trainees cut hair at reasonable prices.

- Accessories like watches, bags and briefcases are also used on a daily basis. They last a lot longer than many clothes, so they're worth choosing carefully and investing in. An interesting, unusual watch is a potent status symbol.

- It's easier and cheaper to look affluent if you don't keep up with fashion. You don't have to think much about clothes if you go for classic dressing. Cords, aran sweaters, kilts and burberrys may be boring, however. They aren't going to match your image if you see yourself as a go-ahead, dynamic type, and they're not much fun if you're interested in clothes.

- Slumps affect the retail business, and bargains can be picked up in the sales. But impose very strict guidelines on what you want to buy so that you're not afflicted by 'sales fever'. Second-hand clothes shops, especially in posh areas of a town, can be a treasure trove.

Dressing Down

The 'My mind's on higher things' look can convey intellectual power and an enquiring mind. We can dress down through looking unobtrusively conformist – just wearing what is expected of us in the situation, with nothing much to express our individuality. This is a look favoured by most of our male politicians. Women sport this look through wearing lots of dark layers – comfortable, cosy and non-sexual. Power is raised through the confident message: 'I'm not particularly interested in outward appearance. I'm sure enough about what I say and do not to have to try to impress or compete through clothes.' Dressing down seems to be a strong trend for the

1990s. This is appropriate for the beginning of a decade in which economic prospects, at the time of writing, are poor.

Fashionability

In contrast with dressing down, keeping up with fashion can be a means of conveying a different type of status. The fashionable say: 'I know what's happening, I keep up with trends, I appreciate the innovative.' Being fashionable also indicates that you are interested in clothes and that you make them a priority in your spending. In recent years designers have realised that a lot more people want to be fashionable at affordable prices – each season another couple of designers bring out 'diffusion' ranges (cheaper mass-marketed versions of their designs, with more emphasis on the casual).

As a fashionable dresser you gain membership to an exclusive and informal club – one whose members can tell an Emma Hope from a Manolo Blahnik (shoes, for those of you not in the know). Of course, like apparent affluence, fashionability can have little connection with style and taste.

The Leisure Look

Your clothes can indicate status through reflecting how you spend your leisure time. Fitness clothing, the tweed jacket and cravat of the weekend gentleman farmer, immaculately manicured nails, impeccable make-up and great attention to the details of clothing reflect what the wearers do or aspire to do with their leisure time.

The Functional Appearance

Clothes, of course, reflect what we do. Jobs are even described in terms of clothing – people used to speak of 'white collar' and 'blue collar' workers. Some of us convey that we see ourselves having more of a decorative than a functional purpose. Clothes give signs about our occupation – male architects and designers wear interesting ties, film directors and actors wear casual clothes indicating that there is little distinction for them between work and leisure, while civil servants are not generally as smartly dressed as people working in the private sector. The quickest way to get a sense of the power of occupational status conveyed through clothes is to walk round a hospital wearing a white coat.

Looking Sexy

Madonna, Joan Collins, Tom Jones and Mel Gibson have undoubtedly raised their status through looking sexy. The journalist Brenda Polan makes the following observation:

> All clothing, once you have protection and modesty out of the way, is about two things: status and sexuality. (And even modesty is about sexuality to a certain extent.) In the past, any kind of shoes conferred status; those who had not went barefoot. But as soon as mankind became skilled enough to make different styles of shoes, the heel had cachet. Worn first by men, initially the heel was functional – it kept a horseman's feet safely in the stirrups. Worn when walking, it showed that you could afford to keep a horse. Ergo, you had status.
>
> Men soon realised that *a.* anything that implied wealth was sexy, and *b.* anything that made you look taller was sexy.

Colour Associations

The colour of clothes can be highly evocative. Purple and gold, for example, are traditionally colours associated with high power. Greys and beiges are not going to increase your visibility effectively.

Distinctive Dressing

To raise your personal power you need to distinguish yourself. Our clothing choices are often influenced by how much we seek to express individuality and how much we seek to fit in, and these needs can come into conflict. People often resolve this by wearing one style at work, and then dressing very differently at home.

As befits an age in which there is increasing emphasis on the individual, many styles of clothing are now 'acceptable'. Comfort and practicality, however, are still not given all the consideration they might be; in many companies, women do not feel it's 'appropriate' to wear trousers.

To be readily identifiable, celebrities often sport distinctive 'uniforms'; they restrict themselves to wearing certain sorts of clothes that emphasise an image. Sir Roy Strong, the writer, historian and flamboyant dresser, was recently quoted as saying, 'I started wearing what I wanted to wear and my career took off.' Perhaps he could not have said the same had he been in banking, but it's my view that people admire displays of individuality more than many of us realise. Sir John Harvey Jones, for instance, the ex-chairman of ICI and now a television star, flouted 'corporate' conventions by sporting loud ties and longish hair.

Carefully chosen so as to suit you, a distinctive 'uniform' that is highly individual can help you gain recognition and increase your personal power. Even if clothes are of little interest to you, it's worth giving some consideration to how they reflect your values, attitudes and standing. You can't prevent other people making interpretations based on how you look. As Oscar Wilde said, 'It is only shallow people who do not judge by appearances.'

chapter eight

POWER AND STATUS – WHO NEEDS IT?

WHAT IS STATUS?

status n. 1. social position, rank, relation to others, relative importance. 2. (Law) person's relation to others as fixed by law. 3. position of affairs.

Concise Oxford Dictionary

S tatus is a provocative word. Few people will openly admit to seeking it. There's a sense that it's not 'genteel' or 'polite' or 'considerate of others' to want to gain status. As we shall see later on in this chapter, status comes in many guises.

Though not openly acknowledging it, I believe almost all of us need and want status. If we use the first definition above, we see that status is to do with where we belong in society, and the significance we are given by others. Only those who choose to live outside society do not regard themselves as having a place within it. We need to form a picture of our society in terms of different groups and our position within those groups to make sense of our world. Some people even find that membership of an oppressed low-status minority gives them a huge sense of purpose in life.

Status is to do with being given recognition for personal power and ability. There is little satisfaction to be gained by knowing yourself that you are good and valuable if others do not appreciate your worth. In many instances, status is the tangible proof of positive feedback.

Some of the 'ologies' – psychology, anthropology and sociology – have each in their different ways defined status. Psychologists describe how the meeting of our 'status needs' – sense of belonging, self-respect and recognition from others – contribute to self-esteem. Since the time when Freud described sex and aggression as innate instincts, a third has been added. Many psychologists and therapists now hold the view that social needs become another instinct. We need our relationships with others, to know our place in society and to strive to fulfil ourselves within it. These needs are all to do with status.

Anthropologists compare the human quest for status with the way status is sought by animals. In *Manwatching* Desmond Morris describes how 'Status Sex' is used by animals and human beings to indicate dominance. He explains how apes and monkeys of either sex display dominance by being 'on top', and how rapists experience a temporary status boost through the humiliation and degradation of their victims. He concludes that 'the Status Displays of ordinary social life have left muscle power behind and have entered the restrained and fascinatingly complex world of verbal exchange and visual ritual'. It is the 'Status Displays of ordinary social life' that are the subject of this chapter.

Status has become a significant word in the twentieth century.
Raymond Williams, *Keywords, a Vocabulary of Culture and Society*

Sociologists consider status in terms of social and cultural groups and interactions. The social scientist Max Weber described status as the prestige and esteem that other people give to an individual and their social position. He differentiated between 'status groups' and 'class groups', considering 'status' to be reflected in a distinctive lifestyle and 'class' to be defined by economic factors. Having a certain amount of money and property can be a condition of entry to a 'status group', but other factors such as occupation, values and beliefs are also important. Weber believed that people's values and beliefs affected change in society. He thought that we are more aware of belonging to a status group than we are of belonging to a certain class. There may be a strong sense that membership of a 'status group' carries with it a sense of exclusivity. Weber wrote about 'status groups' who all shared the same 'status situation', and he believed that these groups played a highly significant role in history.

Certainly India at the present moment confirms this theory. The caste system in that country defines what you wear (colours, styles of moustache, type of knot used to tie your turban), the job you do, whom you marry and where you live. It even dictates what colour you can paint your house: in some places only high-caste Brahmins are allowed to paint their houses blue, to complement their blue clothes and jewellery. The lowest caste are known as untouchables and have low-status jobs like road-sweeping and stitching shoes. Low-caste members have to remove their shoes when they pass a high-caste member, their children must sit on the floor in school and they cannot use the same teacups as higher castes in local tea-houses. But caste status does not always reflect economic status. In some areas market forces and demand for their services have meant that low-caste groups have become affluent.

Successive governments in India have attempted to break down the caste system, only to meet with violent resistance. When the former Prime Minister V.P. Singh attempted to introduce a system of reserving jobs in government for the lower castes he met with riots. High-caste students declared a caste war, with some demonstrators setting themselves alight in protest. The situation is still unresolved at the time of writing.

In Britain, the 1980s could be interpreted in terms of the story of the changing fortunes of a much-publicised status group: the yuppies.

THE STINK OF STATUS

In 1988 a new magazine appeared on the shelves. Glorifying the eighties' values of 'greed is good' as exemplified in films like *Wall Street*, this publication was entitled *Status UK* and its absurd slogan was 'For people with lots of money'. Like a lot of upmarket publications, *Status UK* was high in price and low in content, the bulk of it glossy adverts. Not surprisingly, in view of its blatant and vulgar appeal to aspiration, the magazine failed. The publisher, one Michael Hornett, turned out to be an undischarged bankrupt, who in attempting to keep the magazine going used fifteen false names, eighteen bogus addresses, nine different company names and twenty-one different bank accounts. When jailing him for five years, Judge Graham Laughton told him, 'Your magazine glorified greed, superficiality, snobbishness and self indulgence. You lived in a fantasy world.'

When I first decided to write about status, I met with mixed reactions. Some people suggested that status was an eighties' preoccupation, associating it with dated status symbols like Filofaxes, portable phones and Rolexes – overt displays of wealth. Other people said that they didn't 'buy into' status and paid no lip service to it – they didn't judge people on their job title, big house or designer clothes. They regarded status as a quality associated with superficial displays of superiority.

Several years ago, when I worked in the theatre, I attended a workshop based on the ideas of a man called Keith Johnstone. The workshop was all about status: the status we give ourselves, how it shifts according to whom we are with, how status can rise or fall during scenes and plays. For tragedy to work we saw that we had to witness a dramatic decline in the status of the main character. Comedy was often based on low-status characters getting the better of high-status ones. We saw that scenes worked really effectively when actors approached exchanges between one another as trade-offs in status.

I moved from the theatre to running training courses on communication and public speaking. Time and time again people would tell me that their difficulties were to do with status. Someone mumbled because they'd moved around the country when they were young and had been held up to ridicule because of the 'funny way they spoke'. Another person enjoyed talking to their peers, but became inarticulate when talking to superiors. Executives who had been suddenly made redundant found they were over-selling themselves at interviews because the change in their status had undermined them. Some women found they came up against hostility and contempt when making presentations to groups of men – that they were regarded as low-status by virtue of their gender. I knew that the shyness I experienced in certain situations was to do with my own notions of status. In the small Welsh town where I was brought up, anyone with an English accent was 'posh' and automatically of higher status. Keith Johnstone had written that 'every movement and inflection implies a status', that 'no action, sound or movement [was] innocent of purpose' and that status 'transactions' became clear when there was a conflict. His comments were as relevant to real life as they were to the theatre.

Status transactions happen constantly, everywhere. When a security guard or doorman is pompously officious, he is playing the high status that he thinks his uniform gives him. When a driver screeches to a halt to allow you to cross a zebra crossing, she or he momentarily plays higher status than you, and chooses to let you cross. When a boss deliberately withholds information from subordinates, she or he may be doing so to protect their own status.

It seemed to me that status was a fascinating subject and I wanted to investigate it further. Why, then, did some people react to the word as they did? Why was it getting a bad press? It occurred to me that a number of points were being overlooked:

- Status is acknowledgement of an individual's value by other people. By no means does status need to be measured in terms of wealth (though in America you could think otherwise). Your value may be measured in terms of how intellectual, cultured, influential or concerned for others you are.

- Each of us gives ourselves status – that is, a sense of relative importance.

- Unless we choose to live outside society as recluses, all of us need recognition, acknowledgement and attention from other people. We need company, approval and encouragement from others. We are sociable beings and need the sense of 'who we are' confirmed by others. This 'who we are' is about believing that we matter, we are important, we have some sense of status. In the opinion of Michael Shea (ex-press secretary to the Queen, who must have had plenty of experience in dealing with status), as stated in his book *Influence*, 'a person's greatest desire is to feel important'.

- The closer the definition of our own status to that given us by others in a situation, the more comfortable we feel. Our status varies according to the people we are with.

- We need to make sense of the society we live in. Our society is based on hierarchies and 'status systems', from the way a school is run, via the government to the health service. We want to know where we are in the pecking order and where we can aspire to.

- In my opinion, human nature drives us to want to be significant and prominent in hierarchies – to want status. These hierarchies may be small units – like the family, for instance. Alongside maternal instincts, the reason why some women have babies is that for the first time in their lives they get a sense of status – they become important and attended to in the role of mother. In larger units, you may get your status needs met through becoming a town councillor or getting on to the board of a major company.

- We give other people status, and this helps clarify our own values and beliefs. We admire people, and they set examples for us to follow or aspire to.

- We make status associations with what's happened in the past. As babies we cry to get attention. As we get older, many of us learn that attention-seeking behaviour is immature and inappropriate: we mustn't make ourselves prominent and noticeable. Some of us connect seeking status and recognition with these messages. We are conditioned into thinking that it's proper to be self-effacing. Unlike the Americans, we British value reticence and reserve.

- Status can also be to do with dominance, submission and power. For many people these words do not have good or comfortable connotations. We like to pretend to be nicer and better than we are a lot of the time. We don't like to admit to wanting power and dominance, though many of us will use the euphemism 'I'd like to be more in control', meaning that we'd like more power over ourselves and/or other people. Some of us have little experience of 'power' being used constructively. We may have extensive experience of power being used destructively, to hurt us. We equate status with power, and regard it as threatening.

- There are two sorts of status. The first sort, active status, is based on talent, personal qualities, skills, ability and achievements, and the recognition of these by others. Anthropologists call this functional status. The second sort, overt status, is based on birth, marriage and high-status behaviour and presentation. This is known in anthropology as non-functional or derived status. Some members of the royal family, for instance, seem to me to be low on active status though high on overt status. On the other hand a skilled chef may be highly ranked in active status among her or his fellow chefs. Much of the time, though, we take one another at face value, and the chef who wishes to reach a wider audience will have to start using high-status behaviour and presentation to do this.

It's just like going for an interview – on paper your history and achievements may give you status in the interviewer's eyes. If you fail to translate these expectations through overt status during the interview, then your chances of getting the job may be lessened. The way people use outer status often instructs us how to react to them.

> When General Electric (USA) looked to see what motivated their research staff, they found that 'recognition' came out top of the list. A person who has done a good piece of work wanted it recognised. Status and recognition are known to be powerful motivators because they are rewards that nourish self-image.
>
> Edward de Bono, *Tactics*

Who needs status? All of us do, in one form or another.

chapter nine

THE SYSTEMS
WE USE

This book is concerned with the way individuals use and abuse personal power and status. To help us do this, I think it's worth considering various status systems we use to organise our values and aspirations. I'll also take a look at some status groups that we may be joining in the 1990s.

STATUS AND CLASS

At the top of the hierarchy of 'status' titles in Britain come the royals and, by association, their close relatives. The Duchess of York's father, Major Ronald Ferguson, is reported by the tabloid press to have visited a 'massage parlour'. There is massive coverage of his indiscretion. Marina Ogilvy, Princess Alexandra's daughter, gets pregnant out of wedlock, falls out with her parents and pleads with the Queen to intervene. She sells her story to *Today* newspaper, and following marriage and the birth of her child poses for pictures wearing thigh-high black leather boots and a mini-skirt.

Marina's much-publicised wedding attracts 70 members of the public, compared to 137 press photographers. It would seem that the media are much more interested in royalty than we are. The royals are showbiz, and their antics provide us with light entertainment. Some of them work hard to utilise their status in acting as ambassadors for Britain and as champions of good causes. When Prince Charles pronounces on environmental causes, his birth-given status and the coverage he gets cause controversy. He uses his prominence to help young people through the activities of the Prince's Trust. His influence, though, is constitutionally confined to that of a figurehead, and many commentators have remarked on how frustrating this must be for him.

The press are constantly watching the royals to check how their behaviour befits their position; and theirs is not a position of real influence and relevance in today's democratic society – their status is based on title and exclusivity. In the event of a hung Parliament in Britain, however, the Queen would in theory hold political power. It is a sign of the times that a right-wing policy unit, the Institute of Economic Affairs, has recently mooted the removal of this political power. It has been suggested that the royals serve as an 'adulation valve' for large sections of the population, giving us something on which to project our fantasies and aspirations. If we didn't have them, we might be in danger of starting to worship our politicians. What a prospect, you may think. . . .

Next to the royals, in the hierarchy of 'status' titles, come the aristocracy. They have declined in influence, though they still carry political power in the House of Lords. Surveys show that the aristocracy still own a great deal of the wealth of the country. A 1990 *Sunday Times* survey compiled by Philip Beresford showed that of the 400 richest people in Britain, 103 were aristocrats and 78 were entitled to sit in the House of Lords.

The aristocracy still own a great deal of land in Britain, passing their estates on intact to eldest sons. In his book *Friends in High Places – Who Runs Britain?* Jeremy Paxman points out that the aristocracy have swapped a sense of duty and obligation to those they support for a preoccupation with the business of running their estates. He concludes: 'The 1980s was the decade in which greed became respectable, and the owners of the great estates did better out of it than most. But if their properties are now no more than businesses, like foundries or amusement arcades, whatever residual legitimacy the old order had has gone.'

The wealthiest aristocrat, with an estimated fortune of £4200 million, is the Duke of Westminster. He combines a strong sense of obligation and philanthropy with ownership of a vast amount of property, including an estate of council flats in Westminster. The lease of these flats stipulates that occupation is reserved for members of the 'working class'. Westminster City Council, however, recently wished to sell them off to private ownership. Lady Porter, leader of the council, went to court to do battle with the Duke; Lady Porter's case rested on the view that the 'working class' no longer existed. This was a case of 'old' money and values fighting the 'new'. Lady Porter is the daughter of Sir Jack Cohen, who rose from a barrow boy to own the Tesco supermarket chain. The judge came down on the side of the Duke, and the properties remain protected for occupation by the 'working class'. In the press, one of the suggested definitions of the term 'working class' was that it described people who didn't – work, that is.

Though the aristocracy's influence is diminished, we still see their values echoed in the 'aspirational lifestyle'. Country house hotels flourish, offering in decor and ambiance a flavour of what it might be like to be an aristo. The huntin', shootin' and fishin' lifestyle is widely aped by the socially aspiring. Magazines like *Tatler* and *Harper's and Queen* are still popular, though their 'society' photographs these days are as likely to be of Ivana Trump as they are of the Duchess of so-and-so. And Debrett's, who publish social directories, are changing their views on who's who: ten years ago it contained details of Barbara Cartland's dentist (fascinating . . .), while for the 1991 edition a determined effort has been made to include the likes of Gazza.

The Queen confers awards on people twice a year, though in reality the recipients of awards are more likely to be chosen by the cabinet office. Mark Thatcher is noteworthy for having got lost in the desert, once. He will inherit Sir Denis Thatcher's title which was given because Denis was married to Margaret. Britain is one of the few countries to have an award system and to many people it seems outmoded and irrelevant.

Today, Britain is often described as a 'classless' society. When he came into office, much was made of Prime Minister John Major's background – the son of a trapeze artist, who left school at sixteen. He was cited as the perfect example of how our society has turned into a meritocracy. It seems odd that someone who is so representative of a common trend should have such a fuss made about his background – but Jeremy Paxman shows that the higher echelons of power and influence in Britain in terms of government are still dominated by old Etonians who went to Oxbridge.

Unlike government, the business world is far more meritocratic. The 1980s were the decade when self-made people created business empires. East End 'barrow boys' moved into the City. Over half the chief executives in Britain today have grammar rather than public school education. 'Class' is to do with birth-right rather than money, and in today's society money has become much more important while 'class' is less so.

In many cases money determines lifestyles, and today these are a more effective way than class of determining social structure. In the marketing business, people are no longer categorised by class but by computer programs that sort them according to 'psychodemographics' and 'geodemographics' – in other words, lifestyle groups and their location. Psychodemographics divide people into categories according to what they buy, where they work, whom they vote for, what cars they drive and where they go on holiday. The geo-ones work out where these particular groups live. Looking at people in terms of status groups gives a far more accurate picture of society than dividing it up in terms of class.

STATUS AND POLITICS

Traditional class demarcation lines have broken down and, in keeping with world trends, the influence of socialism is waning. In 1979 just over 13 million people in Britain belonged to trade unions. In 1988 that figure was down to just over 10 million. Sixty-six per cent of the population now own their own homes, compared to 52 per cent a decade ago. Though the Tory party still retains much support from 'old money', its choice of leaders is based on merit and popular appeal rather than class origins. Its policies hold a strong attraction for a status group, the high achievers.

A 1990 survey by the Economic and Social Research Council showed that the average Labour party member was a home-owning professional earning £18,500 a year, with less than a quarter of the membership declaring themselves to be 'working-class'. Despite this, for some people it still seems important to refer to class divisions. In the same year as the survey was conducted, Neil Kinnock was quoted as commenting: 'The working-class people of Bootle expect us to present and dress ourselves in the best possible way.'

The Labour party's image-makers have worked hard to build up appeal to various status groups – homeowners, the self-employed and small business people. When PR companies target voters, considerations of 'status groups' in terms of lifestyle and aspirations are much more significant than the old class divisions.

192

Plato suggested that the people most equipped to be politicians should go into politics with the greatest reluctance. That way, their motivation was likely to be less questionable. Enoch Powell expressed the view that almost all politicians fail ultimately – that is, they suffer defeat at the hands of the opposition and the electorate, or are farmed off 'upstairs' to the House of Lords. Ex-politicians go on to make their living by writing their memoirs and/or newspaper columns, by becoming TV personalities or by being taken on as directors or consultants in business.

Do our leaders and representatives in Parliament deserve to be given status? On training courses, I describe techniques that politicians use to avoid giving direct answers. People often laugh in recognition of the ploys. Few of us pay real attention to our politicians' windy rhetoric – we've heard so much of it that we're anaesthetised. We might assume, then, that one of the reasons that makes people go into politics is because they like talking.

Two young girls from Cardiff, Elisabeth and Catherine Slater, wrote to all our MPs asking them: 'Why did you want to become an MP?' The replies were reproduced in four volumes, offered by Sotheby's as a prize to a competition in aid of the BBC's 'Children in Need' appeal. The answers were interesting, ranging from the ones that suggested purely altruistic motives:

My love of Britain and my desire to try to do something for my country.   *Margaret Thatcher*

To do good and resist evil.   *Tony Benn*

Because I wanted to stop a third world war.   *Dennis Healey*

To serve both the people and the convictions which made me politically active in the first place.   *Neil Kinnock*

to the more amusing and perhaps more honest:

I was no good at anything else, and it is the only job you can do without any training.   *Robert Atkins*

Politics is too important to be left, simply, to anyone else.
                                                    Michael Heseltine

I was mad, suffered from delusions of grandeur and a limited imagination and was ill equipped to do a real job. I decided to stay on in the hope of becoming famous on television once the coverage starts.   *Austin Mitchell*

and finally from John Major

I could not bear to be outside the goldfish bowl looking in.

The irresistible rise of the most innocuous-looking minnow, perhaps.

People who become politicians must be motivated by a sense of ambition and personal power alongside more obviously altruistic motives. Tony Blair and Michael Portillo are often suspected of having more ambition than is 'appropriate'. But so what? They work long hours, have to develop a strong sense of pragmatism, and their motives, actions and opinions are subject to a great deal of public scrutiny. Some politicians have very fine minds and a strong sense of public duty. They seek status and, if they do their jobs well, then in my opinion they deserve it. If they attempt to pull the wool over our eyes in television interviews, then it's the interviewer's job to become more skilled in digging away at the truth. We have the ballot box to demonstrate our objections to them. Are those who pour scorn on politicians a little scared perhaps of drowning in the goldfish bowl themselves?

THE STATUS SEX

- Forty-five per cent of the country's workforce are women.
- 4 per cent of middle and senior management are women.
- Just over 1 per cent of top management are women. (Statistics above from a National Economic Development Office report, November 1990).
- On average, women's salaries are two-thirds those of men.

The status of women has risen considerably since the 1960s, and we can anticipate further progress in the next decade. The skills' shortage that has been forecast means that enlightened employers are already doing all they can to provide facilities to attract women back to work.

But there is still a great deal more that can be done to improve the status of women, especially at work. Economic provisions and pressures work best. In America, discrimination against women at work has been dramatically reduced by the imposition of very heavy fines, which make the paltry sums awarded in Britain in such cases appear grossly inadequate. Ann Hopkins, discriminated against in becoming a partner in the USA division of the international accountancy firm, Price Waterhouse, because she was 'abrasive and overbearing', 'too macho' and considered to walk, talk and dress in a way inappropriate to her gender, won £400,000 compensation in a Washington court room. Heavy penalties against discrimination over here would act as an effective deterrent.

High-status women are accepted in American culture. In the TV show *LA Law* we see believable, ambitious and powerful female attorneys. In Britain the closest we get are tacky caricatures of businesswomen in series like the BBC's *Howard's Way*. The home-grown serials featuring high status women as central characters are usually comedies, so we don't have to take them too seriously.

Role models of high-status women are scarce, and the messages they send out are confusing. Margaret Thatcher acted as a role model, though she was criticised by some for doing little to promote women actively. But she may have thought that positively discriminating in favour of women would make her susceptible to criticism. She enjoyed the prominence of her gender and enhanced it through dressing in bright colours and by paying obvious attention to detail in her grooming. She was able to dedicate herself to her career during motherhood because she married a rich man. Many female high achievers do not have children.

In my view, women have as strong an urge as men to be influential and to achieve goals. Women also have the aggressive instincts that are necessary for survival and advancement. In both sexes this need not be restricted to work, but can be extended to the family, community and leisure interests. Role stereotypes, though, can affect the way in which men and women behave in pursuit of these goals. Some women are frustrated in their quest by a fear of appearing competitive and aggressive, stereotypically 'masculine' traits. On the other hand, a man who goes to work in a predominantly female environment may find that he needs to tone down a blatantly aggressive style and adopt a more co-operative, empathetic one.

Women and men can increase their status by becoming more adaptable in their behaviour and by understanding styles of influence (see Chapter One). To do this, it helps to learn how 'status' works. I have found as great a need to do this in individual men as in women. It's just that in general women, black people and the disabled still encounter prejudice and categorisation as 'low-status' more often than your average white able-bodied heterosexual male.

It's often said that men are more status-conscious than women. They like cars and gadgets that reflect their status. Isn't the traditional housewife concerned with a bigger house, designer kids' clothes or a fine display of ruched curtains playing the status game? Status play is not confined to one sex or the other.

STATUS SYMBOLS AND MONEY

ATTENTION: Wearers of Rolex Watches
In recent months, scores of people have been robbed, beaten, and at least on two instances, even murdered by bandits intent on stealing their Rolex watches. According to Lt Bill Curtis of the Beverly Hills Police Department, robbery and acts of violence involving Rolex products are up significantly. This year, to date, the Beverly Hills Police Department has recorded 83 such incidents. Not limited to Los Angeles, these violent acts directed towards Rolex owners are fast becoming a national menace.

Warning circulated to Rolex owners, reproduced in the
Sunday Times, 9 September 1990

Alongside the 'Rolex' robberies, at that time the American press also carried alarming reports of 'trainer' crimes – instances where the wearers of expensive 'status symbol' training shoes had been mugged for their footwear. In the USA, money is the most effective way of displaying your status. Ivana Trump, Pat Kluge and Nan Kemper are the doyennes of society because they're loaded. Money rather than intellect and culture, is the currency of getting higher up in the pecking order.

In Britain, overt displays of wealth are still considered by many to be vulgar. They offend our sensibilities. Many of us enjoy witnessing the demise of a character like the Rolex-wearing, grossly salaried Sir Ralph Halpern – much too flash for his own good.

Richard Branson, dressed in homely sweater and jeans, always at the ready to clean up litter or fly hostages home from Iraq, is far more acceptable. Culture, intellect, good manners and public service are all qualities that are valued in gaining status. Perhaps our wider appreciation of what creates status – placing values on qualities other than wealth – prevents our society degenerating to the levels of greed-motivated violence as seen in America. Yet we can be as greedy for status through displays of intellectual or cultural superiority as we can be through ostentatious displays of wealth. It can be high status to expound endlessly upon chaos theory and the new physics, to tirade about a review in the *Times Literary Supplement* and to air your views about the latest opera at Glyndebourne.

As a *tangible* measure of your own status, though, you can't beat money. Richard Branson may not *look* wealthy, and he used to live modestly on a houseboat, but it's worth remembering that as well as a music company and an airline he owns a Caribbean island, Necker, which he rents out when not in residence. If we're going to use culture as a measure of status, then Jackie Collins and Cilla Black probably don't rate too highly. With money as our measure, though, Jackie comes in very high with an estimated fortune of £18 million, and Cilla's not doing too badly with an estimated £12 million.

Money can buy the symbols of a high-status lifestyle. Methods of transport can convey your status; the helicopter business is booming as a way of travel for those wishing to move on from their chauffeur-driven limousines. When you're seen eating in the latest overpriced Japanese restaurant, your flexible friend is paving your path to increased status. That skiing holiday you just had in Chile, or your weekend in Reykjavik, let people know that you deserve the status of someone 'who knows where it's at'. Of course, taste, discrimination and awareness also play a part. . . . After all, we are British. Whatever the criteria, though, we still seek status.

The house you live in, your clothes, your car, your accessories and your home furnishings all provide indications to others about your status. We are enticed into consuming by our needs for status and to identify with certain groups. Status is also to do with territory and space. When you buy a weekend country cottage or a big flash motor you occupy more of these. Open space office planning has declined in popularity because people need privacy and a sense of status; you don't get that when everyone's pitching in together at uniform-size and -style 'work stations'. The effectiveness of the symbols we use depends on the audience. Your country cottage may impress your colleagues at work, but to the locals in the village you may be an unwelcome nuisance. Status is most definitely in the eye of the beholder.

The age of conspicuous consumption is said to be over. It's not fashionable to be flashily wealthy any more. But having become consumerist, it's doubtful that we'll change that quickly. 'Retail therapy' makes you feels so good. If we've still got the money, then we'll spend it. It's just that we'll consume different things, because the media will be telling us they're good for us and we know other people who are spending their money in like fashion. Those of us who had Filofaxes and portable phones in the 1980s are now buying finger digital blood pressure monitors to keep a check on stress, designer baby clothes and water purifiers. What next, I wonder?

STATUS IN THE 1990s

Status now means individuality and helping people or animals or trees or rivers or ozone.

Isabel Andrews, writing in the *Observer*

Style is dead! Awareness is in! Let's save the planet! Have we really said goodbye to that dominant eighties' status group, the yuppies? Or are they lurking underground waiting to reinvent themselves in some other terrifying guise?

We are constantly informed about the shifts in values and attitudes that are occurring in the 1990s. *Megatrends 2000*, a hugely positive look at future trends by John Naisbitt and Patricia Aburdene, predicts a booming global economy, an arts renaissance, a decade of women in leadership and the triumph of the individual. Everyone knows that the eighties' 'greed is good' philosophy is out, but where are we going in the nineties? What status groups will we belong to? Here are some suggestions.

The Nouveaux Pauvres

These are the people who talked about mortgage prices at dinner parties through a large part of the 1980s. They're now stuck in a house they would never have chosen to live in, apart from the fact that it was 'a good investment'. Nouveaux Pauvres are determined to put a brave face on their new status. They still hold dinner parties but, creating a trend, they're serving *cuisine paysanne*. Expect shepherd's pie, toad-in-the-hole and pasta accompanied by cider and beer. The conversation will be bound to focus on the 'craft revival' they're involved in. That means they're doing DIY, dress-making and decorating. They've discovered Kaffe Fassett, so they've both taken up knitting – and aren't their sweaters great?

And 'green is good' means that they can recycle just about everything. Fortunately, having had to sell the country cottage, they've discovered the outdoors – in Britain, that is. They did Thailand and Turkey in the 1980s, but with baby Tabitha's arrival a touring holiday in the Cotswolds or Scottish Highlands, looking at all the wonderful trees, is much more fun. The change in circumstances is a blessing in disguise to the Nouveaux Pauvres – they were never really comfortable with all that money anyway. . . .

The Europhiles

Members of this status group are pragmatists. Unlike the majority of people, they could see that going into Europe was important and that they could cash in. They've spent the last five years investing their money in 'self-europisation'. They've learnt three languages and accumulated investment dressing from Giorgio Armani. They spend their holidays touring the Dordogne, the Rhineland and Umbria in the BMW, but now that their language skills and specialised knowledge of Europe have got them promotion they can invest in that farmhouse they fancied in Normandy. They know the difference between a hard and a soft écu when they see one.

Europhiles have strange habits; they like to sit close to you after eating garlic-laden meals, and you'll notice them breathing heavily. Don't worry – it's all part of their 'desensitisation programme'. As part of this you'll quite often catch them washing down bangers for breakfast with a few pints of lager and humming themes from *The Sound of Music*. They live in modern flats with a concierge and

Italian furniture, and their spare toilet bag is always packed. In their fridges there's pesto, sauerkraut, chorizo sausage and a really special Sauvignon blanc.

The Ordinaries

This group follow the leader. In the 1980s the women wore air hostess suits to look like Mrs T, while the men got red braces, striped shirts and swept their hair back, hoping to look like Michael Douglas – but if not, Cecil Parkinson would do. The Ordinaries have two children and they live in suburbia. They are eminently sensible and buy all the family's clothes at Marks and Spencer. They wear a lot of grey and blue. The Ordinaries come from humble origins, and by being as inoffensive as possible they've managed to get on in the world. These are serious people who read books on economics and go to the opera. You're not likely to be invited round to dinner – the Ordinaries are not keen on entertaining. Life is much too austere and earnest to do anything as flamboyant as that. When Ordinaries go on holiday, they usually go to a friend of a friend's apartment somewhere in Spain, and it's strictly self-catering. It wouldn't be proper to do anything too extravagant. Mrs Ordinary belongs to a status sub-group – the maternalists. These old-fashioned women secretly believe that a woman's place is in the home, as a loving wife and mother. They're embarrassed by flamboyant celebrities who champion their cause to get a bit of hype for a book. The Ordinaries make good friends – thoroughly reliable, and always on hand with advice on where to get a good plumber or which building society is offering the best interest rates.

The Deprivation Junkies

These people are big on self-improvement, food allergies, herb tea, tofu and personal trainers. Deprivation Junkies are big on 'alternative' and 'new age'. They wear white a lot and get a regular supply of noxious potions from their Chinese homeopath. Junkies don't smoke, drink or eat flesh, but they do practise Buddism, yoga and reflexology. They're keen on drinking expensive fizzy water with ginseng and guarana extracts, and once a month they go to a flotation tank. Deprivation Junkies are keen on causes, but they make sure that they're OK first. Their bodies are their temples and their minds are OK because their gestalt therapist, chanting, positive affirmations, chaos theory or crystals are sorting that out. These people know the meaning of life: self-restraint and discipline. If there is a hiccup, they can always join an excessives anonymous support group.

Deprivation Junkies holiday in India or remote 'new age' communities in Scotland or Cornwall. They're hard work over dinner – they'll be trying to convert you to their latest cause, and their organic, low-cholesterol, high-fibre, yin and yang meal may well give you flatulence. You've been warned.

The Closet Consumers

Oh dear. These people just can't adapt to the 'new age'. They discovered the joys and benefits of retail therapy in the 1980s and now they can't stop shopping. Their idea of exercise is to stroll through Joseph, Conran and Harrods, gathering up as much as their credit card limit will allow them. Shopping for them is a quick fix of gratification. Before becoming closet consumers they went through a period of shock when, glued to their sofas in front of *thirtysomething* and *Twin Peaks*, they realised that their time was over. The period was known as the era of the couch potato.

The horrible truth dawned on closet consumers that they needed to make more money. So many of them have taken to working from home. Their overheads are low and they can work long hours without being regarded by others as a 'workaholic'. They can sneak out on shopping binges when there aren't many people around. After all, if you work from home you've got to make sure you get out of the house some time. Their home offices are equipped with every gadget going – a good excuse for some shopping, on the grounds that it makes them work more efficiently. They pretend that they don't leave the house much.

Closet Consumers like going on holiday to America, that giant shopping mall across the Atlantic. There they can be truly open about their inclinations. They'll always be wearing something new, but will conceal it under last year's jacket or dismiss any compliments with 'This old thing?' Closet Consumers are good to have dinner with; they'll have used the excuse of finding number three oysters as a reason for visiting the 'better parts' of town.

TO SUM UP

The individual's status is a sign that he belongs with his social group, his badge of emotional security.
Adapted from Charles Handy, *Understanding Organizations*

The harder it is to do something, to reach someone, to accomplish a task, the more we value it when we get there. Psychologists talk about 'cognitive dissonance' – distress caused by there being too wide a gap between what we want and what we are able to get.

The harder it is to join a status group, the more we value it when we get there. You can understand how the nouveaux riches, having striven hard to make money, then want to flash it. It means far more than if they had been born into it. The more exclusive the group, the greater the feeling of status. To paraphrase Groucho Marx: Would you be mad keen to join any club that pleaded with you to become a member?

READING LIST

Berne, Eric *Games People Play* (Penguin)

Bryce, Lee *The Influential Woman* (Piatkus)

Davies, Philippa *Total Confidence* (Piatkus)

Davies, Philippa *Your Total Image* (Piatkus)

de Bono, Edward *Tactics* (Fontana)

Deal, Terence and Allen Kennedy *Corporate Cultures* (Addison-Wesley, now out of print)

Handy, Charles B. *Understanding Organizations* (Penguin)

Harris, Thomas *I'm OK, You're OK* (Arrow)

Johnstone, Keith *Impro* (Methuen)

Kovel, Joel *A Complete Guide to Therapy* (Penguin)

Lewis, Dr David *The Secret Language of Success* (Corgi)

Lurie, Alison *The Language of Clothes* (Bloomsbury)

Masson, Jeffrey *Against Therapy* (Fontana)

Morea, Peter *Personality* (Penguin)

Morris, Desmond *Manwatching* (Grafton)

Naisbitt, John and Patricia Aburdene *Megatrends 2000* (Sidgwick and Jackson)

Paxman, Jeremy *Friends in High Places* (Penguin)

Peters, Tom and Robert Waterman *In Search of Excellence* (HarperCollins)

Rogers, Carl *On Becoming a Person* (Constable)

Rouse, Elizabeth *Understanding Fashion* (BSP Professional Books)

Rowe, Dorothy *Beyond Fear* (Fontana)

Shea, Michael *Influence* (Sphere)

Skynner, Robin and John Cleese *Families and How to Survive Them* (Mandarin)

Stafford-Clark, David *What Freud Really Said* (Penguin)

Storr, Anthony *Human Aggression* (Penguin), *The School of Genius* (André Deutsch)

Williams, Raymond *Keywords* (Fontana)

INDEX